Emilia Juan Bue

Jack in the Navy

By the same author:
Jack in the Pulpit

'Has the rich country flavour of James Herriot's vet books –
a marvellously comic new book.'
NEWCASTLE JOURNAL

'Brimful of rib-tickling tales, told by a man with a ready wit
and a fluent writing style.'
NORTHUMBERLAND GAZETTE

'A jolly good read and a real tonic!'
CLIVE JACOBS 'SUNDAY' BBC RADIO 4

'A great book from one of the north's great characters.'
BBC TELEVISION

'Everyone should have a copy of this book for Christmas'
LIBBY PURVES 'MIDWEEK' BBC RADIO 4

Jack in the Navy
memories of a naval chaplain

Illustrated by Henry Brewis

Bridge Studios
Morpeth
Northumberland
1988

First published in Great Britain in 1988

by Bridge Studios,
4B Bridge Street,
Morpeth,
Northumberland,
NE61 1NB.

Tel.: 0670 518101/519561

© Jack Richardson 1988
Illustrations © Bridge Studios 1988

All rights reserved. No part of this publication may be reproduced, stored in a retrieval system or transmitted in any form or by any means, electronic, mechanical, photocopying, recording or otherwise, without the prior permission of Bridge Studios.

ISBN 0 9512630 1 3

Printed in Great Britain by Hindson Print Ltd,
Newcastle upon Tyne.

Jack in the Navy

Reverend John Richardson, better known as Jack, was educated at St Aidan's Theological College, Cheshire and ordained in Durham Cathedral in 1948. In his ministry he served both at sea and in country parishes. Before ordination he was in the Royal Navy, his first ship being HMS *Hood*.

He then served in the R.N. as a chaplain and is proud of the fact that he had a watchkeeping certificate for both navigation and engineering and was also a 'sin bosun' — the term for a naval padre.

After leaving the Royal Navy he worked for the Missions to Seamen and was also Senior Chaplain, R.N.R. His parishes were all in the north east of England — Wearside, Teesside and Northumberland. He was also Chaplain to the Earl of Durham.

In 1970 he was awarded the O.B.E. for services to the Royal Navy.

Now retired, he is busier than ever writing. This is his second book — his first book *Jack in the Pulpit* was a best seller.

Foreword

One of my earliest memories is of being photographed. Was it an omen that I was dressed in a white, sailor's suit, with blue collar and three white tapes, a black silk, lanyard, white socks and battleship built boots? My twin, Christine, and I flanked my seated mother. I was barely five years old.

The photographer had the solemnity and dress of a funeral director. His contraption was mounted on uncertain sheerlegs; his studio as bright as a chapel of rest and people whispered in hallowed tones so as not to disturb the focus. He intoned chant-like as his head submerged beneath the black shroud which shielded his photographic plates from the tide of light.

'Watch the birdie', he commanded.

He then rendered this manoeuvre impossible by blinding us as he flashed his magnesium flare. I never did see the birdie. Was it a seagull or maybe an albatross?

The navy? Seafaring? From where did the urge originate? Father was army.

Good looking but yet stern, disciplined features and a defiant military moustache he was the proud recipient of the Croix de Guerre (Belgium) and the Military Medal. He put the fear of hell into the Boers, harassed the Huns and demolished recruits. He knew the army drillbook backwards and drilled his family in the fashion of the Fighting Fifth. Yet all his sons served in various branches of the Royal Navy and his daughter, my twin, in the Wrens. His sister's sons were all seafaring and my own family of two sons and a daughter served with the navy.

Deep from the past, energizing and directing us from Heaven where there is no more sea our illustrious ancestor Sir Richard Grenville, a direct ancestor of my father's mother, made sure that he still had some shot in his locker and stirred the waters of our minds seawards.

So impelled by tradition, beguiled by salt water, I eventually strengthened Great Britain's sea bastions by increasing her naval personnel.

I did not originally enlist as a 'sin bosun'. Being what I now realize was a 'nominal' Christian I was not very concerned about religion although I always said my daily prayers. A ship's engine room always seemed to be my idea of heaven and most of my first spell in the senior service was served as an engineer officer. I remained as such throughout the Second World War.

Down in the engine room I saw the light. The telegraphs from the Heavenly Bridge demanded 'Full ahead' and I really experienced a definite calling. When the war was over I responded by seeking early release so that I could commence theological studies. At St. Aidan's theological college, together with other ex-service men, we revised the Thirty Nine Articles of Religion, almost made the principal change course to become a Buddhist, and added Queen's regulations and Admiralty instructions as an appendix to Holy Scripture.

I was ordained at Durham in September 1948.

After a curacy which could have cured me of my 'God-bothering' and a spell as private chaplain to a belted earl I belted back to sea.

I became 'Chaplain R.N.' and my nickname in the navy changed from 'plumber' to 'Bish.' A fuller account of why I changed course is given in the chapter, 'The Reason Why.'

I thoroughly enjoyed my time in the service both as an engineer and a chaplain and had numerous adventures and unusual experiences into which I have delved for this book.

Navy Days

Ventis Secundis

'Dad, did they really hang a monkey at Hartlepool?'

Paul, my youngest son asked the question as I walked with Christine from the kitchen garden towards the rose lawn where Paul and Malcolm sat enjoying the early season sunshine. I had been using a cultivator given to me by my doctor but would have been happier if he had combined the gift with a prescription for embrocation or a weed-killer.

'Watch out, Dad; you almost trod on Jimmy,' exclaimed a startled daughter.

'Who's Jimmy?' I asked, bewildered.

She took up a slimy, grey slug from the garden path and reassured it with maternal mutterings. Carefully she turned it over, thoroughly examined it and said, 'It isn't Jimmy.'

She carefully laid the anonymous mollusc under a bush safe from the crunch of my naval-surplus boots.

We reached my sons.

'Dad, did you hear me? Did they...?'

'Of course not', interjected Malcolm, 'it's sitting here beside me.'

There ensued a scuffle but it was only monkey-play.

I began to answer.

'I really don't know, but as the legend has persisted I reckon that something like that did happen in the Napoleonic wars. I can tell you a true story about a monkey we had on board *Hood*.

I sank down to the grass beside the boys while Christine assured herself that no creepy-crawley was in danger before she too settled to hear my yarn. My first ship was *Hood*. She

1

remains, in my opinion, the most graceful warship ever designed. I joined her at Portsmouth.

Pompey dockyard seemed to be a maze of tangled hawsers, wires and springs with bollards cunningly placed to impede any direct land passage towards a berth. *Hood* dwarfed the nearby signal tower. Not far away *Victory* was vanquished in a forest of crosstrees and cranes. I felt like a Jonah being swallowed up in the mysterious innards of a huge, steel whale. That first night with *Hood* still secured alongside I was seasick. Grenville turned in his grave.

Hood had a ship's pet; a monkey. On Sundays it was dressed in uniform; seamen's rig so as not to confuse it with the master-at-arms.

We cruised north of Gibraltar at a gentle rate of knots enjoying the warmth of the air which came from the Mediterranean. The rig of the day for non-working parties was white uniforms. The first lieutenant decided to take advantage of the lack of wind and ordered the top mainmast to be painted. The very top was a buff white in accordance with naval practice. The seamen had just begun to paint the grey part. They were aloft in their cradles, the pots of paint swaying slightly. So was the monkey. Below on the sanctity of the scrupulously scrubbed quarter-deck strutted officers and the commander, Rory O'Connor. The latter was, as usual, immaculate with a brightly burnished telescope under his left arm. The monkey, unimpeded by any visual aid, employed its limbs in a more energetic fashion. It upset a tin of paint as it performed a Tarzan stunt from one stay to another. In a fine grey rain, the paint freckled the faces and uniforms of the elite. The offender was duly arraigned before its judges. Other offences were taken into consideration. It was well and eloquently defended by the prisoner's friend, its advocate, but alas the counsel hailed from Hartlepool.

Our monkey was found guilty and sentenced to the only punishment for what was accounted as treason or at the best sabotage. It was put in the condemned cell. No one on board volunteered to be hangman or to form a firing squad.

An appeal was lodged after consultation with the monkey and the sentenced reviewed and changed to 'custodial prevention'. Eventually, on arrival in the U.K. it found freedom in a zoo.

Our compass communicated to us that we were on a south-westerley course which was to convey us comfortably over the placid bosom of the Bay of Biscay. Its tranquillity lulled us into a false sense of stability but as we sailed off the coast of Portugal the lights of St. Elmo warned us of the storm to come.

The crosstrees topping our masts became luminous and as the darkness descended they glowed with a weird, ghostly and ominous light, like crosses foretelling the Day of Judgement. The lights had for centuries put the fear of Davy Jones' locker into countless mariners.

3

A force ten gale, developing into a hurricane, endeavoured to change the geography of the Azores. The combined Home and Mediterranean fleets attempted to maintain their own appointed geography. Hammered by the restlessness of an unrelenting sea, *Hood*, which was then the largest warship in the world, sustained damage running into many thousands of pounds including the loss of a strip of armour plating, which was eighteen inches thick, from the forward turret. Despite the rigging of lifelines on the upper deck, injuries were reported and life on board was terribly uncomfortable. There was ample food below decks but few takers. I had been seasick when *Hood* was alongside the jetty in Portsmouth Harbour, yet in the tumult of those angry seas I revelled in good health and appetite!

The storm raged for nine days.

During the First Dog Watch I mounted to the flag deck. From there I could see *Renown* and *Repulse* astern of us battling to maintain their station in line ahead. All other accompanying ships were hidden in a seething cauldron of water. *Hood* wallowed like a pregnant whale. I clung to a handrail, dressed in sou' wester, oilskin and seaboots. The ancient mariner who surfaced from the wheelhouse was similarly clad.

'Good evening, young fellow.' he greeted me, 'Shipping it green,' he observed as our bows dipped low and were smothered in resisting water.

Then he began chatting to me.

His tales were of coal-burning ships, of wooden hulks with both engines and sails. His stories were racey and full blooded. He told me fantastic yarns of the First World War, of German Q-boats, high seas raiders, of Corruna and Falklands and of the beginnings of the Fleet Air Arm.

To me his stories were exciting, so full of descriptive imagination that I regarded some of them as delightful exaggerations. I slipped in a few of my own improbable tales.

For three successive evenings during the Dog Watches he came up and we swapped yarns, while the rain and salt water ran down our faces and the storm continued.

On the fourth evening the navigation officer said to me;

'You seem to be getting on well with the old man.'

'He is a quaint old fellow. You should hear the yarns he expects me to swallow. Who is he?' I asked.

The navigation officer looked shocked.

'Don't you know? He's the admiral!'

Admiral 'Jimmy' James was, as a boy, the original model for the Pears Soap famous painting 'Bubbles'. His nickname in the fleet was 'Bubbles'. He was now admiral commanding the Battle Cruiser Squadron.

He arrived 'up-top' that evening. I sprang to attention. He looked disappointed. 'So they told you. Pity,' he sighed, and I never saw him again until we tied up in Pompey.

I remember getting a blast from the commander, Rory O'Connor, for giving the Boy Scouts' salute as I went on the hallowed planking of *Hood's* quarter deck. Rory went down with his ship, *Pepperpot Penelope*, after writing a glorious page in the annals of naval history.

Our sailor King had graced the throne for twenty five years. He almost didn't make it, for when visiting my neck of the woods to open the new Tyne Bridge the dampness or pollution or both rose from the waters of the Tyne and congested his lungs. As a schoolboy I was waving at him and Queen Mary as they drove over the sacred river but suffered no ill-effects as the lungs of Geordies are immune to the hordes of infectious germs which saturate that river's atmosphere.

So, for the Silver Jubilee, warships of all nations assembled at Spithead with *Hood* taking pride of place. Over a period of weeks, thousands of gallons of battleship grey paint had replaced the existing coats which had been laboriously and blasphemously chipped away. Wire scrubbers and deck scrubbers had been worn down as *Hood* took on a new mantle of gleaming splendour.

The great day came. *Victoria and Albert* sailed majestically between the saluting ships, and hearts of oak rejoiced when the King ordered the signal to be hoisted from the yardarm, 'SPLICE THE MAIN BRACE.'

Now I reckon that Tommy Woodrow, the BBC radio commentator had his share of Nelson's blood that day for at night he shocked Auntie BBC and delighted millions of radio listeners. As darkness covered the water of Spithead all the lights of the gathered ships were extinguished and the ships' companies took up manning positions. All were supplied with torches which were to be lighted at a given signal. I was on the flag deck of *Hood* scared stiff in case my torch would fail to ignite. Then the executive signal was made.

My torch, as did a thousand others, sprang into flaming light which was reflected in the sea. Tommy Woodrow shouted excitedly into his microphone and the ears of ten million listeners,

'The bloody fleet's lit up!'

The lights were out . . . completely. We were 'darken ship' off the Portuguese coast and in 'line ahead' formation, *Hood* leading *Renown* and *Repulse*.

'Increase speed to twenty knots'. The command was given, but not the executive signal which would activate the command. *Renown* made the mistake; I may be biased; and increased her speed before the executive signal had been made.

Suddenly, out of the darkness, a seaman right aft on *Hood* saw the massive hulk of a battle cruiser bearing down upon him as if intent on coming inboard.

Rooted to the spot in fear or desperation?

Not at all. He took action. Hastily grabbing a broomshank he sought to ward off the forty thousand tons displacement hurtling upon him at twenty knots. Despite the broomshank a collision occurred. Both captains faced courts martial . . . and were promoted.

Hood was one of the happiest ships in which I ever served. She will remain with affection among my most treasured memories.

One of the saddest days of my life was when I heard of

her destruction. I was near to the Faroe Islands serving in *Glengyle* when the devastating news broke upon us. The sky was heavy with rain and snowclouds with visibility almost nil and the day was miserable. Perhaps it was weeping for a gallant lady. I was the only personal mourner on board although the entire navy as well as the nation sorrowed.

I still, perhaps irrationally, refuse to accept that *Bismark* sank *Hood*. I heard a report, which I must admit was not official, that *Hood*, eager to win against such a formidable foe, involuntarily contributed to her own destruction. Did it happen in this way?

In order to increase and maintain a high firing rate on her secondary armament, shells were removed from their protective 'Clarkson' cases which were designed to shield them from the backflash of the guns. A line of exposed shells led from the battery to the magazine. Did a backflash set off a chain action of destruction?

I find it difficult to accept that the *Bismark* hit *Hood* and rather incredulous that a lucky shot went down a funnel. Whatever happened left a permanent wound in my memories.

'Ventis Secundis' – second to none, I still believe.

Remorse

Mussolini, like a fighting cock, had strutted across the land of the Abyssinians. The Ethiopians had met this Goliath bearing, like David, slings and stones and in some actual cases, arrows, and they did so well with their antiquated weapons that the Italians came to believe that their opponents had rifles which could fire round corners. What should have been a short, decisive campaign for the Italians became bogged down into a long, drawn-out, disastrous and dishonourable endurance which at times threatened to explode into an Eastern Mediterranean Armageddon. So

Great Britain deemed it wise to have a strong presence in that flash-point area and concentrated her fleet in Alexandria. Flexing her muscles still further Britain decided to demonstrate her punch and sent me to Egypt.

She was known in the fleet as 'Remorse' yet to me *Resource* was a happy ship. She was a floating engineering factory, capable of carrying out tasks both commonplace and challenging. In those days she was an engineer's paradise with the only drawback that she rarely ventured out of harbour. We were moored inside the mole facing the royal palace of Ras-el-Tin.

Faud was king of Egypt and on several occasions my telescope was focused on him as he walked to enjoy the sense of security afforded him by a strong British fleet.

Squid was not a fish but my shipmate. He was definitely squid-like in proportions but he exuded goodwill and common sense.

A poster, brilliantly coloured to divert anyone from an intended course, dominated the canteen flat notice board. It proclaimed the forthcoming fleet athletics and invited entrants to such a varied number of contests ranging from wrestling to tossing the caber, that one had visions of a highland gathering on the fringes of the Sahara.

'What are you entering for, high diving or putting the shot?' teased Squid.

'Nothing if I can get away with it. What about you?' I replied.

I considered his ample proportions and ruled out aquatic events.

'There would be a tidal wave if you dived. If you can bend your knees what about weight lifting?' I challenged Squid.

'You're so skinny you should enter the sprint,' quipped my shipmate.

'Well, I've always fancied myself as a runner. My mother maintained that I never walked but always ran. She used to relate that as a child I made no effort to stand even when my twin sister stood up, wobbled and walked. For a further three weeks I polished my posterior as I propelled my shuffling hulk from one wet spot to another. Then suddenly I stood up, wobbled and ran.'

'That makes you good for the 440 yards,' remarked Squid as he wrote my name on the entry form.

'I'll spur you on from the sidelines', he encouraged.

At all liberty times I was eager to go ashore for training. The venue was the Greek Stadium. Giving substance to the truism that everywhere one goes one is sure to meet a Geordie, the manager of the stadium was a Tynesider called Moffatt.

The day of the race arrived. Armed with spiked running shoes which were wrapped in a towel I climbed into the liberty boat hoping that I could emulate the Flying Finn. The tram scheduled to pass the stadium was moving away as I sprinted to board it. It consisted of two toast racks and a boxed-in contraption secured to the stern. It gathered speed. So did I.

'Hey, wait for me' I yelled as my outstretched hand gripped the rail of the end car. I swung myself inboard. Two, long benches running fore and aft were occupied by women. I squeezed myself alongside an oversized Cleopatra who was reluctant to give space for even a grain of sand and looked at me as if I had one of the plagues inflicted upon Pharaoh, or came from Jerusalem. The double row of yashmaks revealed dark eyes, some disapproving, some definitely hostile, some curious and a few giggling. I felt disconcerted and would have looked out of the windows had there been any. It was a wooden prison!

The conductor entered our coach to collect fares. With my ackers at the ready I became the object of his wrath. He was berserk, falling into a frenzied fit of double-Dutch which was no doubt Egyptian profanities.

It was all Greek to me, until he stopped the tram, hauled my corrugated backside from the wooden bench, took me outside and indicated the legend inscribed upon the carside in both English and Egyptian.

'Harem'.

It was a 'women only' car.

Relegated to the precarious appendage of a toast rack footboard I clung for dear life until the safe haven of the Greek Stadium hove in sight. Somewhere in Alexandria some dusty, little urchin was enjoying his newly acquired running shoes and a loincloth that was an admiralty-pattern white towel, for some son of the Nile had whipped my gear during my transfer from the Harem.

Geordie Moffatt came to my rescue.

'What size do you take?' he enquired.

'Sevens'.

'I've only got eight upwards. Wear them. Here's a pair of thick socks to make them fit,' he offered helpfully.

Geordie handed me a pair of stockings which had probably been knitted by some mothers' meeting for the forces operating in the arctic. They were knee-length and stiff.

'I'd rather run bare foot', I protested.

'Not here, you don't. You'd have tetanus within five minutes. Ah, here's a six. Try them,'

They warped my feet so I settled for eights and thermal socks!

I won both my heats and ran in the final. I finished a well beaten second but sadly the winner was disqualified for an infringement at the start. I really felt sorry for the lad who had beaten me but was proud of my time.

Resource was responsible for the manning and maintenance of a fleet ocean-going tug which did duty in the harbour fussing large battleships such as *Valiant*, *Queen*

Elizabeth and *Barham* to their moorings and occasionally going outside to escort or help vessels into the harbour. It was not long before I found myself doing a month's stint aboard her. I enjoyed it as it was a relaxation from naval routine and discipline.

We were duty tug. It was a Saturday evening. Suddenly we received an urgent command to go to the assistance of S.S. *Ethel Radcliffe*, a collier aground on a sandspit outside the harbour. She was from Newcastle and I reckon that the ship's company had been more interested in the football results than in navigation and because Newcastle United had been defeated had buried their ship's bows deep in the submerged sand. Ostrich-like she was stuck hard and fast.

With thoughts of possible salvage money we cast off fore and aft and with the telegraphs at full speed cut a direct course towards the stricken vessel. I was working out what my share of the salvage money might amount to when I was summoned to the wheelhouse. While there I could see the stranded *Ethel Radcliffe* silhouetted against a setting sun and managed to take a photograph of her. With astonishing rapidity another silhouette destroyed the beauty of the sunset. Coming up from astern a Dutch tug, much more powerful that we were, soon showed us the wash of her wake. The race for salvage pickings was on. Our skipper profaned the evening air and the Dutch flag and nationals. He urged more speed and the engineers, spurred on by avarice and worldly desire, gave it to him. Our tug creaked and groaned as we began to make up seaway.

'Bosun, have two lines ready,' the skipper commanded.

'Aye, aye, sir,' as four lines were prepared as an insurance against failure.

'Heave,' ordered the captain.

The Dutchman had taken up station on the far starboard side of the collier while we lay off her stern. Like an uncoiling snake our line hissed across the short, intervening space. A blind man could have hit the ship. Our seaman was not blind and he missed.

'Another line quickly,' was unnecessary for already a second line cut through the air.

It landed where it should have done but the Geordie seaman failed to hold or secure it. With agonizing slowness the rope evaded all obstacles and fell into the water. As our third rope whistled through the air the Dutchman's rope had been caught and secured. Harrods, Fortnum and Masons and the NAAFI were now beyond our reach.

The Negus

Enterprise was due to follow us into Haifa carrying the rescued Emperor of Abyssinia, Haile Selassie. An Italian tramp ship had been ordered out of the harbour and lay just outside the three mile limit.

In defiance her crew had painted in very large letters on her port side, 'Viva il Duce'.

In those days Britain stood for no nonsense and a determined destroyer sped towards the insulting ship and ordered the offending words to be obliterated. In double quick time the Italians erased the slogan and were escorted northwards under the watchful eye of the destroyer.

I joined *Enterprise* and met the Negus. He was accompanied by his wife, numerous bairns, warriors whose names were all prefixed with 'Ras', his priest, dog and imperial gamp. He was every inch regal even though he had few inches.

Enterprise had to face one hazard. The Abyssinians not having our standards of hygiene used to spit anywhere and everywhere; on the deck, bulkheads, on furnishings in their accommodation and even on the consecrated planking of the quarterdeck. Two seamen were in constant attendance with a bucket and mop.

The first thrill of stepping on the ground of the Holy Land was heightened by the sight from the jetty of *Despatch* altering course to enter harbour. I knew that she was my brother's ship but had not expected to see her here. The next day Charlie and I went ashore together. We walked round the old town of Haifa in preference to the hot, dullness of the modern town. It was fascinating and full of history. We had a meal in a small bar-cum-cafe near to the docks. The next day *Despatch* sailed.

I longed to climb up Mount Carmel. There is an easy track to the top. Four of us perspired as we gently tackled its slope. On the alleged site of the cave in which Elijah hid and was fed by the ravens, the Coptic Church had built a monastery. Visitors were welcomed. Elijah had freely received sustenance while in exile there so the Coptic monks gave all visitors refreshments free of charge. It consisted of a warm, home-brewed and rather sickly ale and a hunk of bread without butter but having a film of honey dulling its brown surface. However, as we left we were directed to a narrow exit at which sat the biggest, heavyweight monk I have ever seen. His begging bowl refused to open as a turnstile until our contributions enriched their coffers.

Our Elijah extractions having been forfeited we returned to the old town and I took my companions into the same eating place I had visited with my brother Charlie. Peacefully munching sandwiches in an effort to eradicate the lingering nausea of Carmel's victuals my teeth almost bit my tongue as the sound of shooting shook everyone there. The owner of the establishment hurried to the front of his premises and hastily hauled down the metal shutter, effectively screening us from the danger outside. Through the small holes in the shutter we watched as Arabs and police fought a street battle within yards of us. The police aimed, not to kill the insurgents but rather to maim them by firing at their bare, sandalled feet. Almost within touching distance of us an Arab aimed his missile of deadly proportions at a policeman who in turn was aiming at the feet of the man. The stone struck the stock of the rifle deflecting the discharged bullet straight to the Arab's chin. It seemed to me an age before the Arab, after standing steadily, finally crashed to the dust in death. He was the first man I saw killed in action.

That afternoon the Negus flew from Jerusalem to London leaving his wife in Palestine which was considered to be a safe place for her. His daughter came to Bath in England and studied to become a nurse. This delightful young princess died not long after the Second World War in England.

Slow boat home.

'Divisions SHUN!'

My recollections were suddenly and dramatically shattered.

A series of loud, echoing booms rattled my cabin. Dashing outside I joined some of my shipmates to watch with great interest from the signal tower and with utter amazement as the Spanish cruiser *Jaime 1* bombarded at point blank range the lighthouse on Europa Point across the Bay of Algeciras. Her huge guns roared in anger and inaccuracy causing cascades of chaos about and behind the lighthouse. Spain was at war with herself. The ratings on board the cruiser had mutinied and landed her officers. Evidently they thought it requisite to close as near as possible to its target and blaze away.

All afternoon we watched the bombardment and as the evening came, the cruiser and the sabbath faded away in a grey, uncertain light. When Monday recalled the light it revealed the lighthouse and the military camp behind it unscathed.

My duties took me in various ships around the Spanish coast.

I was not in *Hunter* when she struck a mine. Her bows were blown off. I watched as she limped stern-first into Gibraltar. Dry docking revealed extensive damage. I cannot remember the exact casualty list but I attended the funeral service held in Gibraltar.

We sighted 'Potato Jones', a merchant captain who was running the Spanish blockade and supplying mainly potatoes to the starving, on more than one occasion but turned a Nelson's eye towards his escapades secretly admiring his daring which was bringing not only lucrative recompense to him but also food to the needy.

I saw my first war refugees.

The frontier between the Rock and La Linea was closed but nightly, Spaniards crossed to Gibraltar in small boats. I walked to St.Michael's cave allegedly the point of entry of the apes from the Barbary coast and saw the pitiful jetsam of human civilian victims of a war that none of them wanted, endeavouring to exist with overturned boats as their only shelter and the generosity of the British their only sustenance.

Sadly for many years I was to see refugees; further numbers from Spain including nuns who were machine

15

gunned as they fled and had nothing but their faith to sustain them; Norwegians; Belgians; Dutch including their Royal family and Arabs.

The clouds hung low over the Rock as *Kent* showed her stern to the bastion. I was taking passage home. She had flush decks all round. To signify that one was about to step on hallowed ground a brass strip delineated the quarter deck. I went aft looking for the strip, saw it, raised my head and arm to salute to find myself face to face with a tiger. I froze. The tiger was evidently equally unprepared for the sight of one terrified and immobile Geordie. It looked at me. I felt mesmerized. I hoped that it had been fed and would not relish Christian meat hopefully recalling that the early martyrs were decimated by lions, not tigers. My fear was removed but timidity remained when I saw a lieutenant approach and lovingly place his arm around it.

My mother had related to me when a boy how, when sitting on a veranda in India on the edge of the jungle she had been confronted by a wild tiger. She kept calm and motionless. She realized that the oil lamp placed there in the evening light was deterring the tiger from further advance.

We passed *Queen Mary* proceeding in the same direction
leaving her behind like the proverbial tortoise. Our speed
was not for bravado. Every ounce was demanded. *Kent*'s
captain after two and a half years in China Seas had
collapsed, a victim of thrombosis. 'Praise the Lord and pass
the ammunition' became 'Praise the Lord and speed those
engines'. We landed him in Plymouth and then carried on
to Portsmouth.

Mourne

Leave is an essential element of a sailor's life. Without it
home life and shipboard relationships would suffer. It is
well recognised by sailors that on returning home on leave
the first question usually asked by friends and associates is
'When are you going back?' After a foreign commission of
two and a half years we are not surprised when on a well
earned spot of leave acquaintances greet us with, 'What,
home again.'

It was August 1939. War clouds had gathered over
Europe but even the pessimists expected them to disperse.
So feeling secure and confident, or perhaps to fool the
enemy, the Admiralty allowed me to proceed on leave.
After four days at home I decided to make a trip to Ireland.

The notorious northern sea crossing lived up to its rough
reputation.

In the vocabulary of seamen we had 'shipped it green' as
the ferry wallowed between Stranraer and Larne. A green,
seasick soldier adhered like a limpet to me almost sweeping
away my sea-legs.

Now the Irish Sea submerged its national colours and lay
benign and beguiling; a deep, almost Mediterranean blue
hardly lapping the sea-wall at Kilkeel, Co.Down. The
colourful flotsam of fishing vessels gently kissed their
neighbour as the barely perceptible sighing of the water

breathed in its slumber.

All was at peace, except in the spit and sawdust end of The Beacon.

'Yin lot are stupid. Ye're back in the Dark Ages.'

The tall, muscle clad man-mountain from Cowgaddens was being sacrilegious in the very shadow of the Mountains of Mourne.

'Aa've heard of your leprechauns and the wearing o' the green, but niver thought aa'd meet actual believers. It's aal e'ewash. Yi've bin kissing the Blarney Stone ower often.'

The regulars of The Beacon were not to be ridiculed.

'It's not the blarney we are talking, Jock. It is fact. Sure, you yourself would not belave even if one of the Little People themselves spake to yi.'

'Och, the Little People themselves. Yi've never seen one, I ken. It's a sin and a disgrace that a six acre field has been left to become a wilderness,' said the Glaswegian who probably only had experienced glimpses of green acres from the top of a tram.

He tossed back a wee dram and began slobbering over a pint of beer. The Irishmen expected him to choke, but he went on;

'Are yi the farmer? What's your name?'

'Patrick O'Hara, and I'm telling yoo, sure enough, that my field is no wilderness. Sure and even now my sheep are grazing in it. De yi hear, lads, a wilderness begorrah. May the saints forgive the man! The Little Folk don't like cattle to be there but don't mind Brenda, my milking cow. To be sure, they like her milk because she is often dry at milking time.'

'Awa' wi' ye. She's gey auld and there's little grass in that field; it's aal stones. Ne wonder the puir aad coo is thin.'

Then he flung out an unwise challenge. As the dregs from his glass gurgled down his throat he wiped a massive hand across his frothing lips and demanded,

'Git me a spade.'

'And what would yi be doing wi' a spade?'

'Aa'll turn over the first sod in that field.'

Duly armed with a spade which was used for digging for rag-worms, and accompanied by a mass of Catholics the heretic entered the field. Anxiously the Irishmen crossed themselves and awaited the thunderbolt. Jock strode to the middle of the six acres, looked around, studied the sod beneath his feet and invoked John Knox, Rabbie Burns and the Boiler Makers' Union. Then dramatically, with pneumatic force and a Bannockburn Bellow, he thrust the blade of the spade through the impeding earth, to strike a submerged boulder and break his ankle.

'To be sure, the saints preserve us, the fairies put the stone there.'

I had arranged to stay for ten days at the farm of Mr O'Hara, which lay about two and a half miles north of Kilkeel.

'Sean has died suddenly. God rest his soul. May he rest in peace.' Patrick crossed himself as he made the announcement. Sean was his farmworker who was only thirty eight years old. He had suffered a coronary attack as he walked homewards up the steepness of the Mourne Mountains.

'Jack, maybe you would like to go and see Sean's wife and have a wee word wi' her. I know that she would appreciate that.'

The farmer's 'maybe' was imperative. I went.

Sheilagh was an attractive woman, with dark eyes and raven hair.

'The boss said yi might call. It is very good of you. Come in.'

The whitewashed house had only two rooms. There was no such luxury as a bathroom as the tin tub hanging outside advertised and the outside bothy testified to the energetic or desperate marathon demanded of the householder with a low capacity bladder.

A storm lantern hanging from a hook spoke of the nocturnal exercises of penance after an evening spent drinking the home-made concoction of fire water distilled in the hut beside the henhouse. It was July. It was hot and I was steaming after the climb up Mourne's lower slopes. A peat fire smouldered in the grate.

'Sit down, Mr Richardson. I'll fetch you a drink. What'll you have?'

'Just an orange drink please.'

'Orange? Oh, I don't think we have any of that.'

I settled for water. It was from a spring and seemed to be a breeding agency for wildlife. Beside the wall behind me was a single bed, and on it lay a sheet-covered body. With my back to it I talked to the widow.

'I have a photo of Sean at our wedding. It is in the other room. I'll bring it.'

After she had left I heard a deep, prolonged sigh come from the recumbent stiffness of the body behind me. My scanty hair lost its curl and stood up on end and my heart after missing several heartbeats broke the sound barrier. Cautiously I turned to look at the bed. There was no movement and no heaving of the chest or twitching of nerves. My nerves jangled but I was tranquillized by the thought that I had allowed my imagination to run wild. Relaxed, I again contemplated the curling smoke from the sultry fire. Like a confirmation of a dreadful resurrection the sigh sounded a second time. I dare not turn around. Sheilagh entered the room carrying a photograph.

'Sheilagh, did the doctor see your husband after his death?'

'Yes. He and the priest came at the same time.'

'Well, will you sit down.'

She sat. I took her hand. The air was heavy and oppressive. The sweat of fear increased my perspiration. The sunshine lost itself behind a cloud while a clock emphasized the passing of time. I sighed on this afternoon of sighing. I gulped, then said, 'While you were in the bedroom the body sighed, not once but twice. It was not my imagination.'

The moment was solemn, my message dreadful and Sheilagh's laugh almost profane.

'Oh, that's not Sean. He is in the mortuary in Kilkeel.

This is my brother. He has travelled all night from Cork and is resting. He cannot sleep in daylight so he has covered his head with the sheet. It is too warm for blankets.'

She woke her brother. Too hot for blankets yet this stopper from Cork had been lying fully clothed and wearing boots.

Before I left Sheilagh said,

'Of course you will come to the wake. All Sean's friends will be here. Get Mr O'Hara to come with you.'

Six o'clock in the evening, with the Mountains of Mourne in shadow and myriads of heavily clogged gnats feasting like vampires on my arms and neck, saw me increasing the gathering mourners to over the fifty mark. Mourne seemed to be mottled with mourners as they assembled on the grass outside the croft.

The sun was still up but moonshine was swilling their innards. The farmer shepherded me into the living room where the dead now had his glory. The coffin stood up against the wall previously occupied by the bed. The upper part of the coffin lid was hinged and hung down like a stable door revealing the features of the dead man. Bronzed with the outdoor life he looked extremely well. Mr O'Hara threw a few coppers into the coffin. My ancestry prevented me following suit. If the dead man was required to pay the ferryman he would have to do so without the contributions of a canny, Calvinistic Caledonian.

A small white haired man picked up a pipe, packed it with tobacco from his own pouch, applied a lucifer and produced a poisonous smog. When the pipe was glowing and I was gasping, the old man said to all and sundry;

'It was his favourite pipe. I'll give him a last pull at it before I claim it for myself.'

Incredibly he endeavoured to force the stem into the dead man's mouth, but evidently there must be a 'No Smoking' sign on the Pearly Gates or 'Smoking Only Within' adorning the portals of perdition, for the dead man kept his teeth clenched.

I had a call from Belfast. I was instructed to return

forthwith to London. Britain's bastions were about to be repaired. After my long journey from Larne to Stranraer and then to Carlisle and on the 'smoke' I ended up at Chatham to receive orders to join *Mooltan*, an armed merchant cruiser, which was in dock in Belfast. So I retraced my steps which led me to Belfast and to war.

n.b.

War

The Boats

Mooltan seemed to enjoy an Indian summer in the comparative safety of Harland and Woolf's shipyard. For six weeks I had little to do. War at sea had begun. *Courageous*, sister ship to *Furious* in which I had served during the Munich crisis, had been sunk. Rumours of the sinkings of many U-boats counterbalanced our early losses and scars. Our ship's company were becoming frustrated and restless as the conversion of the ship ate into days, weeks and a second month. My accommodation was spacious and to me palatial. I grew familiar with Falls Road and its opposing sides and coloured doors. I liked Belfast and the people there did great things for us.

We were warned to remain strictly neutral in subjects political and religious.

Early on a good Sabbath day before the Irish segmented themselves into papists and presbyterians *Mooltan* slid down the lough in to the Irish Sea. All look-out and gunnery stations were manned. Odd splutters from our oerlikon guns temporarily diverted the course of our convoy of seagulls. The forenoon was mainly occupied in executing U-turns and S-bends. Having felt our sealegs and settled down comfortably after lunch our relaxation was rudely disturbed by the klaxon summoning everyone to action stations. The enemy had not been sighted. A full gunnery exercise was to be carried out. As our guns spoke out individually one felt a sense, not only of security, but of satisfaction for at least we had the power to throw something back at an attacker.

Then we fired a broadside. Every gun on the starboard side opened up creating confusion in the sky and turmoil on board. The planking on the upper deck corrugated itself, companion ladders severed connections and the engines shifted as in a nightmare from the beds to go out of alignment with the propeller shafts. It was a quiet sabbath evening when the good Scots pounded the paths to their places of worship and *Mooltan* limped into the Clyde. The fresh air from the distant hills of the north mingled with the tang of the sea, and an artist's sunset behind us tinged everything with the mellowness of a balmy autumn evening. Church bells, not yet silenced, sounded melodiously over the waters of Clyde as we moved to a mooring buoy. It was a night of peace and thoughts of home, which after all, for me was only three hours away.

For five days rumours swept the messdecks. Then all the ship's company were sent home for indefinite leave except me. I was drafted to Harwich and the Third Submarine Flotilla.

'Icebox' as *Cyclops* was affectionately known in naval circles, brooded like a grey hen on a watery nest alongside the quay at Parkstone. Her chicks were nine little submarines. Being approximately 600 tons displacement each, they looked like fledglings but in their chirping and pecking these S-class boats showed skill, seamanship and success. When not on patrol they returned to the warmth and shelter of mother hen *Cyclops*. The latter had been captured by us in 1916. She had been a German grain carrier and we converted her into a depot ship. Between the two wars she had shown the flag at Freetown and it was said by matelots that before she could be brought home she had to be floated from an undersea mountain of condensed milk tins.

Sterlet torpedoed a German cargo ship in the Skagerrak and picked up the entire crew before crash diving to avoid an enemy fighter plane. Alarmed at being on board a submarine, the twenty five survivors were further terrified at the thought of becoming prisoners-of-war. The Nazi propaganda machine had instilled into them the false fear that as prisoners-of-war they would find no adherence to the Geneva Convention but that the British would torture and starve them and survival would be very uncertain.

For the remainder of the patrol we sought to reassure them and they were duly handed over to *Cyclops*. They spent two pleasant days and three nights in comparative freedom being well fed and able to join with our sailors in recreation and films in the sheds on the quay. On the third day they were assembled on the well deck for departure. We wished them well and gave them sweets, cigarettes, woollies and magazines and even, illegally, money. The assurance they had gained from us that their imminent internment was nothing to be dreaded must have seemed to be flagrant mockery or deceit as an engine shunting three coaches came alongside. The first and third coaches bristled with soldiers carrying rifles and fixed bayonets.

Singly the Germans were escorted by the military to the train and we were saddened that such an unnecessary and misleading display of military might had been employed.

Sterlet was the first of our flotilla to be lost. Then followed *Salmon* after an outstanding patrol when she had encountered and engaged a large German naval force. *Seal* humanely and sensibly surrendered after destroying all confidential papers and equipment.

A parachute was observed by army units as it fell into the sea off Harwich one evening. *Greyhound* and *Gypsy* sailed to investigate. The foremost destroyer passed over the reported position releasing the magnetic mine which came to the surface to demolish the bows of *Gypsy*. She sank in shallow water. It was the first magnetic mine dropped by the Germans and it was intended for one of our submarines. Britain responded to this new and deadly weapon by degaussing our ships. The following morning as we sailed we passed the grim sight of *Gypsy*'s masts protruding from her watery grave, a grim reminder that we were dealing with a callous and unscrupulous foe.

Seamen swore and sweated on the quayside. Bollards were being painted white, sheds scrubbed out, the starboard side of *Cyclops* smartened up and the engine grease and horse manure scraped from between the railway lines. Prince George, Duke of Kent, was due on board for lunch. We had converted one of the sheds into the Mermaid Theatre and I had painted a mermaid on either side of the stage.

Prince George came in, looked around and said,

'They are the only mermaids that I have ever seen who had square backsides.'

I wondered how many mermaids he had seen!

On board *Cyclops* he visited the messdecks chatting with all and sundry, winning the approval of those disgruntled toilers of the forenoon. All their exertions suddenly seemed to be worthwhile. He descended into the depths of *Sea Lion*.

After lunching extremely well with Captain Ruck-Keen he went rather unsteadily over the gangway to take his place behind the steering wheel of the official car, the chauffeur and aide occupying the rear seats. Our hearts failed us as he literally took off and yet drove along the quayside, which was a maze of bollards, hawsers, drains and loco lines, with great skill and we all watched with admiration. He was gracious, interested, friendly, a man among men and he

26

boosted our morale. Three weeks later he was killed as his aircraft crashed over northern Scotland.

British intelligence was always weeks astern of that of the Lower Deck. Long before it was whispered officially, hairy matelots industriously applying Palmolive soap to their steaming bodies had communicated between their zinc, round, portable, admiralty-pattern bath tubs that the Huns intended to carry out an air strike against our flotilla. Whether or not our agents heard of it in Lisbon or in the Salvation Army hostel at Harwich action was taken and taken speedily.

The sheds ashore became hives of industry as craftsmen and sailors worked together to construct a flotilla of wood and canvas submarines. Within forty eight hours these mock vessels, looking every inch like the real thing, were moored in midstream of the River Stour but away from harbour installations and population. The same evening, under a cloak of uncertain light *Cyclops* led the way into the North Sea. I was aboard her and we were accompanied by five submarines. Our top speed was six knots. Our freeboard was so excessive that even in the subdued seas we wallowed like a pregnant walrus. A thick mist obliterated *Gypsy*'s grave and muffled the cry of the gulls and shrouded everything beyond five yards of our bows in mystery. The next day we heard jubilant, treacherous Haw Haw revel in the news that Germany's air might had knocked seven bells out of the Third Submarine Flotilla.

The voyage north was slow and hazardous. A minefield stretched from John O'Groats to Dover and we had to remain shoreside of it in the days before radar and in the gloom of the persistent mist. No one knew the outcome of hostilities or whether we would, as individuals, survive, but our determination and resolve was strengthened, for while off the Yorkshire coast we heard Winston Churchill give his 'blood, sweat, toil and tears' speech over the radio. So we took the future as it came; a day at a time.

Flat Bottomed

I was now with Combined Operations. Our training centre was on Hayling Island. Our accommodation was holiday chalets which were better suited for tropical delights of prolonged droughts than the inclement uncertainties of the coast-line of the English Channel. The roofs were as effective as wide mesh wire netting. The walls were so flimsy that one could hear one's neighbour change his mind. The paths outside were unmade and wooden duck-boards provided walkways. It seemed while we were there that a prolonged rainy season saturated every day, so seaboots and oilskins were the normal rig-of-the-day.

'You are to take your crew to Littlehampton by truck and bring back an A.L.C. by sea. Sub Lieutenant Williamson will skipper a second boat and you will be in overall charge.'

'Yes sir,' I saluted the commander.

He was a man of few words, although if his anger was roused his vocabulary increased tenfold.

Chalky White, my coxswain was not too keen.

'Look at the weather, sir, it's blowing a force ten gale.'

It certainly was blowing and the sea was full of white horses but they were being driven, in my estimation, by a force seven wind.

'Get the lads together, Chalky, and assemble at the transport office,' I ordered.

The road journey, via Havant and Bognor Regis was a dull thirty miles. We arrived at the Harbour Master's office. The men dodged through torrents of rain to the dockside canteen.

'You'll not be going out in this in your flat bottomed boats,' commented the Harbour Master.

He was a fatherly figure, comfortable in size and manner. His weathered face had obviously been beaten by many a storm at sea and no doubt he spoke now with wisdom gained from experience.

'Fraid we've got to,' I replied.

28

'Then you'd better wait a while and see what the weather does, although I can't see any hope of improvement. Care for a cup of tea?'

'I don't drink tea,' I replied, 'but I'm sure that Bill would welcome a cup.'

Bill, was Lieutenant Williamson whose Christian name was Herbert.

'OK.' said the Harbour Master, 'And I do have some cocoa here. Care for that?'

The wind increased as did our fears. The rain drove almost horizontally across the small harbour to splash in miniature floods against the window panes. Sipping cocoa, I looked outside. The two landing craft struggled at their moorings. The sea was in chaos. The clouds scuttled themselves across the turbulent surface of a tortured sea.

'It's force nine now,' said the Harbour Master, 'I'll ring up your commander and recommend postponement of the sailing.'

'No, I will. I'll speak to him. It would be better. Get him for me on the phone.'

'Like bloody hell you will,' shouted the commander so loudly that he hardly had need to use a phone.

The adjectives flew as he continued,

'What do you think you are running? A bus depot? Get those bleeding craft at sea immediately.'

I felt that it was alright for him speaking as he was from a warm, stable and carpeted office and no doubt very near to the whisky bottle.

I repeated his remarks, minus the swearwords, to the Harbour Master.

'Then I'll not give you permission to leave harbour and my word is law here. It would be suicide out there. Hang on. I'll ring the met. office.'

He exchanged pleasantries with the met. men and then said, 'It is now officially force ten and increasing. Visibility is poor and clouds lowering. I cannot let you go. I'll ring the commander.'

The latter's invectives were plainly audible for all to hear.

My cocoa ruffled and Bill spluttered.

'The man's mad,' said the Harbour Master. 'He insists that you sail. I have done what I can. It's up to you now.'

I looked towards the sea. It made me sick to look. In a blast of wind I was propelled to the canteen where the lads, confident that they would not be sailing, sat around pints and Dolly birds. I was truly sorry to spoil their fun but I gathered them together, thankful that the craft carried extra fuel.

'We'll never get past the breakwater,' protested Chalky. The two crews made no secret of their support for him and their opinion of the commander, but they were not mutinous and soon we edged our noses beyond the breakwater.

I led the way. Progress was slow. The sea, tide and wind combined in opposition to us. Soon, despite all our efforts we were going crabwise eastwards.

The flat bottomed boats leapt about crazily, refusing rudder or correction. The last I saw of Bill's boat was when it capsized. I endeavoured to turn to his assistance without avail. I almost hazarded my own craft in the manoeuvre. We carried no wireless and would not have been allowed to use it if we had. Chalky wrestled with the wheel while the other lads furiously pumped ship. If we had tried to correct our course we would have turned over.

Very slowly and in greater travail than a woman in childbirth we were on a course for France which was enemy occupied territory. The darkness veiled the chaos and the sea, out of vision, roared and tossed in a destructive mood. We endured the night fearing every moment.

The dawn came and so did an abatement of the wind. The sea still ran high and hard but our craft responded to our rudder. We had no bearing but steered west-norwest by compass. By early afternoon we sighted the Nab Tower. Going through the Witterings we met a rescue boat. It closed and informed us that it was searching for the rescue boat that was searching for us.

Safely ashore we awaited word concerning Bill's boat.

The commander sent for me. He informed that Bill's craft had ended up on the shingle near Angmering. All its crew received hospital treatment but were not detained.

I received a blast for querying the commander's orders.

Dog Collared

Although the future, jealous of its secrets, breaks in single waves upon the shore of time, a full tide flooded the vision of Edith Gardner-Williams and a revelation was made known to me.

'You are requested to go to the ship's office, sir,' said my steward.

When I arrived there I found five other officers arraigned before the desk, who were to be my friends and companions for most of the war. They were Lieutenants Robinson, Rowley, Rogers, Forman and McCulloch.

The paymaster, a lieutenant commander recalled from retirement for the duration, was a pleasant man and his Pickwickian personality beamed benevolently upon us as if we were his kith and kin.

'Mrs Gardner-Williams is a millionaire's widow.' he began.

We were suitably impressed not merely because such species were rare in those days but because it was obvious that she was about to be involved with us.

The paybob continued.

'She leased a house near Havant from the Marquis of Tavistock with the intention of offering it as accommodation for pilots at the nearby fighter station. She did this because her son is stationed there. The R.A.F. has turned down the offer because of the nature of the duties there which involve scrambling. So she has offered it to us. You'll be the first officers to go. Be ready by 1800. You'll have dinner at Warblington House. You lucky people!'

Dinner over, we sat in the library. It was a magnificent room. The walls were lined with well indicated volumes and on a low table was an ample supply of liquid refreshment. I had selected a book and settled into a comfortable armchair. The greatest joy seemed to be the warmth and sight of a living fire although the provision of fresh milk came a close second.

Despite my interest in the page I became acutely aware of a gaze and lifted my eyes to see Edith, as she wished us to call her, looking stedfastly at me. She met my gaze and leaned forward.

'You will wear a clerical collar,' she said in a low whisper.

Astonished I said, 'How do you know?'

'I've just seen one form around your neck,' was her reply.

She refused to be drawn into further conversation. I had not then considered taking Holy Orders and I sat no longer able to concentrate on my reading. I willed my companions to go to bed. Near midnight the last 'Goodnight' was said.

Edith drew her chair nearer to mine.

'Well, they've all gone. What do you want to know?' she

asked.

I was bursting with curiosity and questions.

She told me that I would survive the war and do well in my subsequent theological examinations.

'How long have you had this gift?' I queried.

'I have not always regarded it as a gift,' she replied, 'I have fought against it. I don't want it. I find it difficult to control.'

'Tell me about it. I'm really interested,'I begged.

'I first noticed it when I was eighteen. With my parents I was visiting an art gallery exhibition. People were standing about drinking wine. I had a soft drink. I noticed a man standing across the room facing us. To my utter astonishment as I looked he seemed to develop a second head. Clearly another head with defined features became apparent behind him. I blinked, hoping that it would go away, but it only vanished as the man came to speak to my father.'

'It must have been particularly startling to a teenage girl,' I remarked.

'No,' she asserted. 'The frightening thing was not the apparition but the realization that I'd seen it.'

'Obviously because of the prediction you have made of me tonight you haven't lost the power. Has this kind of thing happened to you very often?'

'Much too frequently,' she replied, 'I now seem to have control over it. It doesn't always involve seeing things. I sense or feel conditions.'

'I don't quite understand. Can you explain to me?' I requested.

'For instance, my husband and I sought a country house,' she began to relate, 'We went to the Cotswolds to view a property. It was splendid outside. The grounds were very well kept and the house offered a picturesque aspect to the south and I was very impressed.

"We'll have it, darling," I said enthusiastically to my husband but he was cautious.

"Hang on a moment," he said, "we haven't looked

inside yet." Together with the agent we mounted the steps that led to the main door. The agent inserted the key and pushed the door open and stood aside to allow me to enter. I was rooted to the spot; absolutely transfixed.'

I broke into the account to ask, 'Why was that?'

She continued.

'I couldn't move or speak for a moment. Then I said firmly and sharply,

"We'll not take it. Let's get away from here as quickly as possible".

"But you've not looked inside and you loved the outside," my husband declared.

"I cannot explain but there is something incredibly evil in there," I protested.'

I had listened intently and then remarked,

'Maybe it was nothing more than a reaction or a sudden whim.'

'Oh, no,' said Edith, 'I was proved to be right.'

'How?' I asked.

Edith continued.

'A retired master of Eton College took the house. After being in it for three months this happened.

"I'm off to bed. Don't be long dear," said the master's wife.

He was sitting in front of the fire reading.

Flicking over a couple of pages he said,

"I've only two pages to read before the end of this chapter, then I'll be right up."

'His wife dozed off only to awake in the early hours of the morning to find that her husband was not in bed. Fearing that he had dropped off to sleep downstairs she descended to find him dead in his chair with an expression of abject terror upon his face. His eyes had bulged, his features distorted and his tongue hung grotesquely from his twisted mouth.'

'Ah,' I said, 'he had suffered a stroke.'

'No,' emphatically asserted Edith. 'Medical evidence showed that was not so. It is, as far as I know, the only

verdict recorded by an English coroner's jury that death
was due to having seen something horrific.'

'Maybe the book scared him,' I ventured.

'I shouldn't think so.' replied Edith, 'It was a text book
on botany.'

About a week later, after breakfast I picked up my mail
from the hall stand when Edith appeared at the head of the
stairs.

'Hold up the packet in your hand,' she requested me.

It did not need a clairvoyant to know that it contained a
photograph, for in large letters was the instruction,
'Photograph. Please do not fold.' I held the packet aloft.

'It is a photograph of a young lady with the initial E.
She's wearing a bee's wing around her neck. You'll marry
her,' Edith said without any hesitation.

I had never mentioned Ethel's name to her previously
and I did not know about the bee's wing.

'If I am right then let me buy you an unbreakable frame
for it.' Edith offered.

She was right. I had to write to Ethel to ask what the
pendant was and she replied that it was a bee's wing set in
crystal. I have the photograph to this day.

The fog hung low over the channel making navigation
and exercise difficult. It intensified as the evening drew on.
Vic Rogers had an old car which we used as transport
between Warblington House and Hayling Island. As we
returned that evening the visibility was practically nil.
Robbie, being the tallest, stuck his head through the
sunshine roof and directed Vic at the wheel. We got into a
crocodile of cars playing at follow my leader. We reached a
roundabout, went around it twice, lost the car we were
following and took the wrong exit. Robbie was frozen.

'Down below,' hailed Robbie, 'I'm frozen up here. Let
somebody else take a spell.'

No one volunteered but as Mac was the most convenient
he was conscripted. Soon Mac from the crow's nest realized
that we were going in the wrong direction. Executing a

blind and dangerous U-turn we found the roundabout again
and managed to escape via the correct exit.

Not far along the road air-raid wardens and members of
the Home Guard had erected a road block. Two German
fighter planes taking advantage of the fog had
indiscriminately machine gunned the road hitting the
crocodile whose tail we had previously wagged. The car
which had preceded us and whose tail-lights had evaded us
on our first encounter with the roundabout was blazing
furiously, its glare turning the surrounding fog into an
incandescent but fearful and dangerous glow. We could
distinguish still figures lying ominously covered at the
roadside. As we waited for permission to proceed we heard
a dull thud muffled by the fog. Thanking our lucky stars
and grateful to Robbie for his misdirection, for
undoubtedly our car would have been hit had we not erred
from the way, we arrived at Warblington House. Edith,
neat and well-ordered as ever, apologized that our meal
would be delayed.

'Come. See what has happened,' she invited.

She led us into the kitchen.

The dull thud we had heard along the road had been the

explosion of a small bomb which had demolished all the outhouses and blasted the kitchen windows outward. No one was hurt but our roast beef became a casualty of war and we ate spam instead.

Some weeks later I sat in the Singapore Room at Warblington House sketching an item of furniture. Edith looked over my shoulder.

'Not bad,' she remarked. 'Would you put something in my sketch book?'

'Of course I will,' I agreed.

She brought it to me. It was leather bound and already contained some splendid sketches and water colours of whose excellence I could never hope to attain, but I knew that I would do my best for such a gracious, unforgettable lady.

I sat on the stairs at Parham House, the Gosport home of a relative, listening to a record playing on the gramophone when Vic came in with the news.

'We're all off to Inveraray in the morning. Ever been there, Jack? It's in your neck of the woods.'

Everything north of Watford was considered to be my neck of the woods.

'Say goodbye and come to Warblington to pack. I have the draft notes and railway warrants so we don't need to go back to Hayling,' informed Vic.

So we left the South. Eventually I sent Edith's sketch book back to her London address in Great Portland Square as she had requested me.

It was returned to me by the Post Office,
'Premises destroyed by enemy action.
Occupant presumed killed'

Campbell Territory

'Ah'm no' having that bearded yin,' vehemently declared

Kirsty. 'Aal men whe wear beards hae' something te hide.'

Edward VIIth, George Vth and Rob Roy all began to rotate in their graves as Kirsty indicated her rejection of the only bearded officer on parade.

Lieutenant Martin Van Heems' Van Dyke adornment bristled in the soft, warm air which relaxed over Inveraray and left the leaves of the trees lanquid in their limpness and, holding its breath, left the unruffled waters of Loch Fyne to finely duplicate the surrounding hills. Martin had increased our numbers to the mystic seven, or, as we liked to think, the magnificent seven. Huddled about us a fling of highlanders gazed like a harangue of hapless haggis. There was Hope and his brother Dodo, Peter Munroe, Dougie McLeod, Bob and John Rose and Miss MacLachlan, alias Kirsty. We stood with the loch behind us facing Kirsty's Temperance Hotel, the only place where one could be sure of a wee dram!

'The navy's here,' John Rose informed Commander Smedley.

He had gone to the Argyll Arms to stem the flow of whiskey down the commander's throat. The latter almost choked when John told him of the arrival of naval personnel, but whiskey being too precious to waste he gulped hard, gasped and had another drink to sustain himself. I think that the commander was a relic of the First World War, still maintaining a naval presence in this northern outpost of Britain. With us came the realization that another conflict had broken out. Our arrival at Inveraray had been totally unexpected. Now we were being selected by the natives for billets. Six of us went to Bob Rose, Martin went, complete with fungus, to Kirsty.

Bob's house was called Dunquach, the Gaelic equivalent to Duniquaich, the hill that lay above the castle and was crowned with a quaint watch tower. Neil Munroe, the noted Scottish author, lived and died next door. He had buried his favourite dog in his rear garden and my window overlooked that grave.

'Collect your things from the Argyll and go to your

billets,' commanded the commander, 'and I'll see you all again at 0930 tomorrow in the same place unless it is raining. Then we'll meet in Kirsty's.'

Bob Forman needed help. He had not quite recovered from being seasick in the back of the army lorry which had brought us up the old 'Rest and be thankful.' Mac helped me to carry his gear and put him to bed. Commander Smedley had told Bob Rose and Kirsty to obtain from the local shops all necessary victuals with the assurance that ration coupons would be supplied. John Rose, Bob's son, legged off to the shop grateful for the opportunity of seeing the girl he had earmarked for the wearing of his tartan. Jenny stood behind a mountain of marmalade. She seemed to be always jammed behind jam and I came to know her as the 'marmalade girl.' Without moving or taking her eyes from the laddie of McBraynes she produced a huge tin of bully beef. John lifted it as if it was as light as a feather and with a lighter heart trod air as he returned to Dunchuach. With the arrows of Eros piercing his heart he pierced the tin and arrowed his thumb. Almost severed, his thumb spurted blood and his Aunt Mima kept repeating, 'Oh my, oh my,' while his mother phoned for the doctor. He was rushed to Furnace, not to be cremated but to receive medical attention. John bore that scar to his dying day and used to laugh as he claimed to be Inveraray's first war casualty. More realistically it was a scar of love which he bore to church when Jenny became his wife. The bully beef had added flavour.

The church spire became the town's second war casualty. It was still puncturing the sky as I turned left to the post office which hid its identity in a large, grey fortress which in turn housed the council chamber and sheriff's court upstairs and the prison cells below.

Going through the correct door I saw a clerk behind a massive counter. Lots of notices warned the Scots that careless talk costs lives and caused them to to be silent as they had no desire to expend anything. The solitary customer already there had come to spend his time rather than his money. I gained this impression when I saw his moulting sporran.

Sir Walter Scott's, Last Minstrel came to my mind.

'His withered cheeks and tresses grey
   seemed to speak of a better day.'

This vagrant had no harp to be carried by an orphan boy and his 'lay' was the query,

'What are you doing in Inveraray?'

Loyal to the posters my reply was both non-committal and evasive. Having obtained an ample supply of 1½d stamps I came outside to find Old Ancient waiting for me.

'Aal walk doon the road wi' ye,' he invited himself.

Propelling an old, rusty bike which creaked in disharmony with his knobbly knees, the kilted scarecrow slowly accompanied me. I prayed fervently that none of my shipmates would see me walking with this impoverished remnant of humanity.

'The last of all the bards was he.'

He certainly barded as we stood looking over the waters of Fyne. I broke the string of yarns.

'The castle looks like something out of a fairy story book. It must be about the most beautiful castle I have ever seen.' I remarked.

'Would you care to see inside?' the old man asked.

His voice sounded more like that of an educated man as he dropped the dialect to ask the question.

'Oh yes. Could you fix it? I don't want to get you into trouble. Do you work there?'

'Off and on,' was his uncertain reply. 'But there's no time like the present. Let's go now.'

So we went forth together; the battered old son of time and the anxious lieutenant. As we approached the main door a retainer opened it.

'I did not get your name,' the old man said.

'Lieutenant Richardson... Jack,' I offered.

'I'm Neil,' the old man said and turning to the big man in the kilt, the little man in the kilt said,

'Brew up some tea.'

'But I don't drink tea,' I said.

'Aye, it's a bit early for a dram. How about coffee?'

'That would do me fine' I replied.

So it was decided and the big man looked down at the smaller.

'Very good, your Grace,' he said as Neil, Duke of Argyll, having left his bike outside, led me bewildered to look around his highland home.

It was he who introduced me to the Episcopal Church of Scotland.

Mac and I called on the Rector. His shock of black hair accentuated his shallow complexion. His deep-set eyes lacked lustre and gave me the impression that had been too long in this Anglican wilderness. He did not seem to be overwhelmed at the prospect of having his congregation increased by 200 percent.

'So the Duke has invited you to come to church on Sunday. You'll not be able to follow the service as he has a liturgy all of his own,' drawled the cleric.

Then as if in the way of compensation or inducement he added,

'We do not take collections.'

The Duke was waiting for us near the bell tower. He was

wearing his Sunday sporran and the symbol of shame, the Campbell tartan. Evidently besides his ox and ass, his bike enjoyed a sabbath respite. I introduced Mac to him and he introduced us to the rites and ceremonies of Neil, which incorporated a Campbell chant intoned in a manner well suited for the cloisters. Our mumbled devotions and his cantata completed we returned to the castle where, after his Grace had said 'grace' we enjoyed a good Sunday lunch.

Years later when Neil died I lost a good friend. It was with a real sense of bereavement that I journeyed to Inveraray to watch his body as it was borne on the waters of Fyne with the Galley Standard flying bravely above it.

He was a gracious, old man but lived in an era when the massacre of Glencoe still rankled among the highlanders. Bob Rose had a housemaid. She was over eighty years old and she was Mary McDonald. Whenever she saw the Duke she passed to the other side in case his shadow fell upon her. Both were godly people and the salt of the earth.

Neither Land nor Sea

The winter came and springtime naturally followed. From the abundance of the blue mist of bluebells in the castle grounds I despatched to my fiancée a goodly collection carefully packed in dampened cottonwool and accompanied in the same box by a dozen Loch Fyne kippers!

During these dark months there were more than seasons which came and went. Service personnel of both navy and army and all connected with Combined Operations increased almost daily at Inveraray.

The admiral lived near Inveraray..A small figure with a tremendous sense of democracy, he endeared himself to, and earned the respect of all ranks. His humanity and sense of humour often kept up our flagging spirits. In the wild fastness of Argyll he often walked about wearing below his naval tunic, a pair of grey flannels and brown shoes.

It had poured with driving rain all day and by evening the clouds had spent their aquatic supply and the sodden earth rejected the superfluity of water, which now lay in muddy pools almost everywhere. An army truck had gurgled its death wish and stood forlorn with the wheels firmly embedded in a large patch of rainwater. The unfortunate driver lay on his back exploring the mysteries of its under-belly and cursing the fact that it had ever been constructed. As he worked with a leaking oil sump anointing his Satanic scowl, a voice pierced the gloom.

'Having trouble?'

He struggled with an obstinate plug as he replied, with expletives, to the effect that he was not exactly gathering bluebells. He could see the lower part of a pair of grey trousers and rather small, brown shoes.

From the heights above in almost apologetic tones a voice advised;

'You'd better look out to see who I am.'

The driver twisted himself free of the chassis and, to quote his own words,

'I saw yards of gold braid.'

'You're very lucky that I am not a young sub-lieutenant,' said the admiral, 'for then you would have been in serious trouble.'

An extra large Munroe shackle was required for the mooring buoy laid for large ships. *Glengyle* already tugged at the only one already in use. *Glenroy* was due to arrive in a couple of days.

The admiral sent for me.

'I have seen some of your chartwork and must ask you if you can do engineering drawing too.'

'Yes,' I assured him, 'and would enjoy doing something like that.'

'Good,' said Admiral Hallet, 'I want you to go to *Glengyle*'s mooring and take the dimensions of the Munroe shackle. Make a sketch of it so that I can get the Royal Engineers to make one at their small foundry. We certainly do not have time to get one made at the dockyards. Do you think that you can manage that?'

'Of course, sir,' I replied, not knowing or anticipating the hazards that lay ahead.

Spibey, my redheaded coxswain was waiting in a small cutter.

'Ken,' I instructed, 'we have to go to *Glengyle* and measure the Munroe shackle. It looks like blowing a storm soon so we had better go there now.'

Ken Spibey brought our little craft expertly alongside *Glengyle*'s gangway and I jumped to it. Quickly ascending because of the blowing wind, I asked the officer-of-the-day for permission to board the buoy and explained my mission. He seemed to be indecisive and even nervous.

'You had better consult with my captain,' he said and then escorted me to the hallowed precincts of the captain's cavernous cabin.

'What do you want?' ungraciously bellowed the Supremo.

His stentorian single syllables bounced to me via the satellite of his bulkhead as he did not turn his head towards me.

Cap in hand I began to explain my mission.

He had only one order for me and it somehow involved a journey to the nether regions on my way 'off my ship.'

Spibey came with me to report to the less fiercesome admiral. The latter laughed, as well he could but I was only a humble lieutenant.

He gave me a letter addressed to *Glengyle*'s captain. Again Spibey ploughed the watery furrows to *Glengyle*. I was spotted.

Two burly seamen descended the gangway and thwarted my attempts to board by warding us off with long boathooks. I tried again and again.

'I've a letter for your captain from the admiral.'

My shouting was wasted on the wintry air.

There was only one thing left to do and I did not hesitate to do it. In a large circle we navigated to the buoy. Dangerously Spibey and I leapt upon it leaving the seaman to keep our boat nearby. As the waters of the loch were by now exceedingly choppy we had to lash ourselves to the securing cable. I took the measurements. Spibey wrote them down with a fountain pen on the inside of a cigarette packet. Constantly the buoy submerged taking us both on downward plunges into the engulfing waters which, just as regularly, obliterated the written measurements, and had us blowing every time we surfaced like whales. I was determined that I would complete the work having gone so far, when a further hazard manifested itself.

Through my sea soaked vision I could see the captain gesticulating from the bows.

'Get off my bloody buoy. I'll have you keel-hauled for this', he shouted among other words.

In his debatable vocabulary he kept yelling at us and approaching from the starboard I noticed a boat coming towards us. Not waiting for further confrontation, Spibey and I scrambled on board our boat and sped ashore. I gave the admiral the measurements and the story and he seemed to appreciate the latter more. The shackle was made and remained there until after the war was over. Every time I saw it I felt rather proud. It was 'my shackle' and no longer a Munroe shackle.

It was not long before I was again summoned to the admiral's desk.

He had his headquarters in Fern Point, a large house near to the pier head, and now used by the Admiralty from which we also obtained our pay. His gold braid rivalled the electrical fittings and his brown shoes blended with the mahogany. As always he was pleasant, though concise, and made our work seem not only interesting but absolutely vital to the war effort. I left him feeling that Churchill, Hallett and Richardson were the greatest obstacles to Hitler's ambitions.

'I do not know if you have any previous experience in this kind of work but I am confident that you can do it. It's not another buoy.' asserted the admiral.

'I want you to co-operate with our civil engineer in the preparation of land for a naval base. It is to be the headquarters of the naval side of Combined Operations,' continued my superior, 'if you go along to Admiralty House you will find that Mr Brown expects you.'

'Sir, I would be delighted to help but I am not a civil engineer. What I can do?'

'We don't expect you to do civil engineering. He has asked for someone who can do the necessary drawings. He will give you all the relevant instructions. I'm sure that you will be of great assistance to him'.

I found the civil engineer, a Geordie of course, a graduate of Durham University and a civilian civil engineer. Together we went to the site which was some two and half miles down the loch towards the sea. The sight of the site alarmed me. It appeared to be an extension of the loch itself for its surface rippled in miniature waves as the wind disturbed it. In seaboots we waded into it.

'Hey, Geordie', I remarked, 'we've both heard of the clarty lonnen but this is impossible. We would need to be either Moses or Joshua to get dry land out of that. It's not as if we could just pull the plug out and see it disappear. It would be easier to merely moor a ship off shore.'

'Oh, I don't know,' mused Geordie. 'It's not really deep. We'll set about planning drains.'

At this he unrolled a survey map of the area and explained.

'The boathouse will be where all this water lies and the living accommodation and admin. block and parade ground up there on the high ground,' he indicated.

I perused his pencil outlines with great interest never believing that anything would ever materialize.

'Ah well, let's begin our survey,' Geordie optimistically suggested.

So while the wind whistled and the rain rebuked our thoughts of drainage we began the initial stages of a camp which was to prove vital to the outcome of the war and which even today bears the noble scars of our efforts, while caravanners cavort on its hardstanding foundations.

'Oh my, oh my, what will we do without you,' bewailed Mima.

'We're only going to *Quebec*, Mima. Dunchuach will become our second home. Dinna fash yersel aboot us. Ye ken we'll be doon here almost every day,' I replied.

'Och, away wi' ye.' stammered Mima through her moistened eyes. Together with Mrs Rose, Bob, John and Mary MacDonald, the maternal Mima, the spinster, the undiscovered treasure, waved us goodbye as the six originals climbed aboard a lorry to be transported, not to Botany Bay, but a mere fifteen minutes walk away to the operations base which I had helped to be built and was now known as HMS *Quebec*.

A young sub-lieutenant was seducing a willing wren in the end cabin of our accommodation hut. His door was wide open. The full operation was for any to witness. I saw, but with a more refined animal lust, hastened to the Wardroom to engage in the seductive delights of the galley's gastronomic, agonizing nosh-up. As usual the sunshine of the evening was liquid and I stood gazing idly, and in a pensive mood at the pattern of raindrops on the small, square window panes. Reflected a hundred times in their global spheres I saw a seaman whose appearance repeatedly clouded the brilliance of the raindrops. He was doubling with a pack on his back, a rifle slung across his right shoulder and was devoid of any protection against the inclemency of the highland weather.

I went out.

'Halt,' I shouted against the wind.

He stopped his concentric marathon.

'What are you doing? Come here out of the rain,' I instructed.

I knew and liked the man. He was in a civilian life a solicitor's clerk. He was well educated and had begun law studies when the war broke out. He contributed much to the social life of the camp, being a member of the orchestra we had formed for concerts. Now he was an able seaman doing his bit for his country and it was sad to see him obviously and surprisingly as a defaulter.

'Well, what is this all about?' I enquired.

'Jankers, sir,' he admitted.

'Jankers? Been in the rattle then? What have you been doing?' I asked.

'The duty officer saw me coming out of the canteen. He accused me of wearing my cap on the back of my head and of giving him a slovenly salute.'

'How long have you been doing this?' I requested.

'About a quarter of an hour, sir. I have to do two hours,' he informed me, 'Well you've done enough. Go back to your mess, have a bath and be careful in future how you wear your cap. I'll put it right with the duty officer,' I said, to his great relief.

I was unaware that Commander Cassidy had heard everything and as I turned he said to me.

'What was all that about?'

So I told him.

'That bloody grocer's assistant. He's more trouble than enough. I wish he was back slicing bacon. Send him to me.'

So the duty officer, a young and new sub-lieutenant who had talked his way from the counter of his local store through a selection board to King Alfred and had been given his first appointment at *Quebec*, stood before an irate commander. I had mixed feelings, however, when I learnt the following morning that the able seaman had been hit by a lorry while on his way to the armoury to return the rifle and had sustained leg injuries. He was in a makeshift hospital in the grounds of Inveraray Castle. I visited him taking with me a precious bar of chocolate and the duty officer. One sweetened the palate; the other sought to heal wounds.

'How about four gallons of petrol?'

This was a tricky request for it came, not from a scrounging stoker or a cadging commander, but from a prayerful padre.

I wanted to be on the Lord's side but my difficulty was to ascertain what exactly was the Divine Will. Would His wrath be kindled against me if I purloined the precious petrol from the storage behind the boathouse or would He smile on mercy and condone the crime because of the underlying motive to motivate the motor of His agent? Was my spirit to be scorched because of spirit?

In the end I followed the directions of that higher authority Commander (E) Bill Shaw and referred the request to him. He had no religious scruples as long as Bacchus satisfied his thirst for the spirit. With great faith and my intercessions the padre presented his petition for petrol to Bill. It was a case of unanswered prayer. The chaplain climbed to his car and headed towards Inveraray but despite all his divine connections the vehicle stuttered an Amen beside the phone kiosk conveniently adjacent to the church. The padre may well have entered the hallowed precincts to seek power from above but instead entered the phone box and reversed a call to us.

'That bloody padre's car has packed up,' fumed the commander sacrilegiously, 'Jack, take a mechanic and see what you can do for him. Hang on a minute, he's practically next door to the George. I'll come with you.'

We left Bill to meditate at the bar while we lifted the car's biretta. There was a smell of incense coming from the carburettor. It was apparent that some religious rite had been performed. Maybe the padre had sprinkled it with holy water or carried out a total immersion baptism, for water flowed above its plimsoll line.

The padre, bless him; as Bill did, in sweet, other-worldly innocence explained. 'Commander Shaw wouldn't let me have any petrol so I thinned down the petrol already in the tank with water.'

As we prepared to tow the car back to the camp I mused that perhaps he had thought that he was driving Balaam's ass or even Jonah's whale but after penance at the bar, even Bill saw the funny side of things. Religion is such a joyous thing.

Stand Fast, Christian Sailors.

Perhaps the joy of religion is hidden at times.

After a hazardous operation across the North Sea *Glenroy* felt the soothing massage of the sun-sparkled waters of Loch Fyne. We crawled past *Quebec* on the port side as we moved to our appointed mooring buoy; the one I had measured. Lieutenant Commander Ross supervised our mooring but neither he nor his crew straddled the buoy as I had done. I was pleased to be afloat again after my stint ashore with *Quebec*. I felt that once more I was truly involved in the conflict.

'Captain requires you in his cabin, sir.'

Accordingly, cap in hand, I searched my conscience for any hint of misdemeanour and presented myself before my lord and master.

'Sit down,' he invited so I knew that I was not guilty.

'I received the daily orders for tomorrow from the admiral's office ashore. As *Glenroy* has just returned from sea we are excused sending a church party ashore to the garrison church. I had thought of having a church in the welldeck but there were so many vehicles stowed there that it would appear to be impracticable. Do you think that it would be a good thing to send ashore a volunteer church party?'

I realized that no matter what my opinion might be, and it was negative, he had decided to send men to church. I didn't know that there was a garrison church ashore.

'Well, sir; I know that the men are expecting a make-and-mend tomorrow. They have been closed up in action stations for days on end and apart from being tired need to get their dhobying done and letters written.' I objected.

'They can do that in the afternoon,' replied the captain, 'and in any case I am giving them a make-and-mend on Tuesday. Put a notice up on the canteen board asking for volunteers and take charge of the party.'

'Yes sir,' I promised without much hope.

By 1800 the blank list testified to the will of the men. The response of the officers was equally negative and I reported to the captain.

'I have already arranged for the church boat to call on *Glenroy* at 1000 hours and I have no wish to cancel it. Go down to the messdeck and use your persuasion,' he told me.

I turned to leave him when he called after me.

'By the way, I'm sorry that I can't go. I'll be busy preparing a report. Do your best.'

Miracles have to be planned.

My inspiration was a piano. Screwed to the deck on the seamen's messdeck its polished varnish had been wiped off by repeated floodings of the concoctions that seamen drank. Its pain at being exercised was audible in its resultant reflexes and its strings sobbed rather than twanged. It was ready for retirement but at the moment was serving not as a musical instrument but a resting place of ditty boxes and beermugs. I lifted the keyboard lid and found a pack of cards. The underside of the upper lid was pasted with lurid pin-ups which left nothing to the imagination.

'Tubby, give us a bash at the piano,' I began.

Tubby loved kippers and always had a fishy smell about him. He was too fat for the battered old piano stool but a bench was cushioned for him and he overflowed it as he contemplated the keyboard. Then he flexed his fingers with sickening cracks, caused a whirlwind by breathing in deeply and began to knock seven bells out of the old Joanna.

The first miracle was to get him to play. The second was the way he played, for soon, accompanied by laughter, the tune of 'Blaydon Races' was discernable, at least to Geordies. His nimble fingers, though podgy, conjured up some stimulating tunes while the unscripted words sung by the seamen had other stimulating connotations.

Gradually we diverted from dirty little ditties to bellicose ballads, until I influenced the singing of hymns. Sailors love to sing hymns.

After the 'Battle hymn of glory' while they were still at their pinnacle of spiritual attainment I canvassed for churchgoers. I assured the men of salvation and a jar at the George. I pleased the captain with over fifty names of ardent worshippers who were at least willing to suffer the travail of a church service if a pub beckoned beyond the Blessing.

'This is more than the requirement when it is compulsory. I'm delighted and will speak to the men myself before they go. Well done,' praised the skipper who was to skip church.

The captain spoke. In gold-badged number ones the men stood at ease awaiting the church boat which could be seen buzzing busily about the ships which were obliged to supply congregation. The maintenance commander ashore was so keen each Sunday to impress the powers-that-be by packing the church with reluctant naval personnel, many who could not differentiate between Moses and Abraham Lincoln – well they both had beards; that I doubt if he left any room for God.

Time flew by and the boat had ignored us. Had the coxswain been instructed to collect a church party from *Glenroy*? Our commander rang ashore and was assured that we would be collected after all the other ships' church parties had been collected.

'New every morning is the love', was the hymn being sung as we finally entered the church, but morning mustn't have broken for the maintenance captain. From a glorious company of apostles, martyrs and prophets which stood in angelic, but strictly hierarchical order around the communion table – we used an old Presbyterian chapel, the captain negated any affirmation of love as his withering stare of condemnation like a poisoned arrow was directed towards us. Quietly gathering in the gallery we bowed our heads in supplication while the names of the damned were

53

entered into the log of the captain's intentions. The sermon was hell-hot but its searing soul-searching was lukewarm compared to the blistering attack bellowed by the maintenance captain.

We had endured the service and thoughts were on the paradise of the bar of the George. We stood getting organized for the march-off outside the church.

'That ship's company stand fast,' yelled the captain cutting the sabbath air asunder, 'and at attention.'

His order, directed towards us was barked before the startled ladies who moments before had been singing 'Love divine, all loves excelling'. They were now experiencing the other side of dualism. Contingents from other ships were smartly marched away. We stood fast as ordered. The captain chatted to the ladies then without a glance towards us shouted over his shoulder,

'You lot stay there until I return.' and went his way to Admiralty House.

He lunched as our sailors stood first on one leg then another counting away the precious drinking minutes until the George closed. That hour passed.

'You can go now,' came the command at 1530.

'No sir, not yet,' was my timid but determined reply.

The captain glared at me. His four gold rings out-dazzled my two but did not dim my resolve. I was now in at the deep end.

'What do you mean?' he demanded.

For the sake of discipline aboard, morale and the church I had to speak.

'With respect, sir, we are a volunteer church party from *Glenroy*'. He interrupted.

'You were late.'

'Let me explain, sir,' was all I asked.

'There can be no excuse. Dismiss your men.'

'Yes sir, but I will have to report this to my captain,' I said.

'Come here!' was his barked command.

I walked to him.

54

'Do I hear right? You are going to report me? What is your name?'

'I am not reporting you, sir. I will have to report our lateness to our captain, and my name is Richardson,' I informed him.

His attitude changed. He almost seemed to soften.

'No need for that, Richardson. I'll have a word with your captain.'

We missed the pub, the liberty boat and our Sunday roast. We got a message to *Glenroy* who sent a landing craft inshore for us. The captain sent for me.

'Must have been a long sermon this morning. I don't mind them having a drink afterwards but to stay in the pub until now is not on. What happened?'

I told him. I let him know how sick I felt about it and how the men felt that they had been let down.

The next morning the maintenance captain came on board, sent by the admiral to apologize to our captain.

Two weeks later Admiral Hallett said to me,

'Tardy with your devotions, Richardson. Don't worry in future for I will not require compulsory church parties from *Glenroy*. I'm sure that your men would rather pray on the fo'c'sle.'

Snow-white

Snow-white was a Geordie. His true surname was Lovely but we could hardly use that. His complexion, where visible, was a permanent grey which no amount of Fuller's Earth could improve or eradicate. There were more bumps on his face than there were hills in Argyll. Tufts of dark hair sprouted from where the razor couldn't reach. The hair on his head was jet black and untameable. I often wondered why he didn't grow a beard. Beard or not, he had a heart of gold and would help anyone at anytime. This was proved to me.

He was the seaman attached to my assault landing craft. We were engaged in forty eight hours of exercises along the shore of the loch and were monitored by brass hats from all three services. I always endeavoured to give the soldiers a dry landing. Blunt bows at right angles to the beach with a dozen yards to go I dropped my kedge anchor astern as the craft ground quietly upon the shingle. Silence and speed were the necessary elements of surprise. Higher up the beachline a bevy of brigadiers and a magnum of admirals were busy assessing another craft. Soon they would turn their attention to my part of the beach. The soldiers went ashore dry and all seemed splendid. I was pleased.

'Right, Snow-white,' I whispered, 'let's get out of here. Pull on the kedge.'

Strongly he pulled and we moved about four yards.

'Kedge cable around the screw, sir.'

Geordie's report was as chilling as the winter's air. Several feet of the cable entwined itself around the propeller. This was the unforgivable sin.

I could see the umpires beginning to walk towards us. The craft began to swing broadside and drift towards stranding.

'Don't worry, sir. I'll attend to it,' Snow-white said in a very low voice.

Without any hesitation he stripped to his underpants and dived into those arctic waters. The wind combined with the iciness of the sea withering us with its sleet-laden assault. I prayed as the big-wigs stopped a little distance away unaware of our predicament. Geordie kept coming to the surface to gasp for breath as he hacked at the cable.

Finally he hauled himself out of the water, the screw turned and we went easily astern, Snow-white's veins stood out blue like motorways on a road map. He dried his shivering limbs with his vest.

'Don't worry about the kedge, sir. We'll come back tomorrow to retrieve it,' he stuttered through his chattering teeth.

H hour was 0200. It was a perfect night for an operation. A slight sea-swell brooded towards the beaches and a concealing, clinging mist conveniently hung as a shroud over our movements. There were ten other ships in our company but we could neither see nor hear the others. *Glenroy* had a list of ten degrees to starboard so all craft commanders on the port side were warned to 'walk' their boats down to sea level. I spoke to my winch hand.

'Lower us gently when the time comes. Take the brake off slowly so as we can ward off the boat from the ship's side with boat hooks. Understand?'

'Yes sir,' whispered the winchman.

'Now you know the signal, don't you?' I queried.

I was deliberately being fussy about all of this as not only was silence not to be broken by a boat hitting the ship's side but there were lives at stake.

'When I give you two tugs at the rope begin lowering,' I continued, 'and once more do it slowly.'

'Aye, aye, sir. You've nothing to worry about,' responded the figure clad in duffle coat and comforts.

All the assault craft had been loaded since 0130 and hung from their strengthened davits loaded with human cargoes. The commandos were in full fighting kit. I wore oilskin, seaboots and lifejacket.

Time donned iron boots and dragged. Waiting is so timeless. The mist placed us in isolation and the world about us would not have existed except for the umbilical cord for signalling. It formed a link with the mother ship.

0200 breathed its belated breath to intensify the mist and the waiting, for nothing happened. One of the purgatories of life is when nothing happens. The vacant minutes began another hour. We hung there, unknowing and silent, with thoughts racing through our heads. I was not worried about what lay ahead.

We were well briefed and prepared. I began to think of loved ones, of faces I wondered if I would ever see again. Once again I played football on the Willows and saw the church steeple piercing the sky. The winch hand was also thinking. He visualized a steaming cup of cocoa in the warmth of his mess and to give substance to his thought he handed over his duties to a relief hand. He went at 0230 and forgot to tell his relief to lower us gently.

The crisis came at 0250. Quietly but distinctly, with a renewed resurrection to matters of the moment, I tugged twice at my twine. The relief winchman responded by releasing the brake to the full. The forward end of my craft dropped dizzily as it shook itself free of the ropes and block while the stern remained secured. Like a vertical pointer to the depths the craft disgorged its camouflaged campaigners into the sea beneath. The forward block, with no restraining burden, swung crazily to hit me on the left side of my head and knock me violently forward as pendulum-like it returned its swing. As I went, one armoured half-door sliced through my seaboot to penetrate behind my shinbone opening up my leg from ankle to knee. I lost consciousness and only felt the cold, engulfing waters as a voice brought me to my senses. Buoyant in my 'Mae West' I was being supported by a seaman. The sweetest tones I have ever heard and the prettiest face I have ever beheld were those of Snow-white.

'You'll be aalreet, sor, divvent worry, aa've got you,' he whispered as he held me firmly.

With his sodden hair floating like uneven seaweed he supported me to a scrambling net. I remember little until I stirred in the sickbay.

'How is Snow-white?' I asked.

The sick bay tiffy was an opposite to Geordie, being effeminate and reeking continually of aftershave, but he was an efficient and good-hearted lad.

'Bring him to me,' I asked, 'and by the way, what is wrong with me?'

'A double fracture of the left ankle and maybe severed nerve in your left temple. I'll go and get Snow-white.' So I said goodbye to *Glenroy* and landed in a ward at Mearnskirk Childrens' hospital near Glasgow.

The Butcher And The Beef

'I'm pleased that it's you and not me.' The hospital porter cheered me up with his gloomy prospect. He was a kindly man but had a countenance and hushed air of confidentiality that was suitable for a funeral undertaker's parlour.

His usual task was to take bodies to the mortuary; he was wheeling me to the doctor's consulting room.

'Why?' I asked, as the wheelchair seemed to traverse innumerable corridors and corners.

'You'll see,' predicted the porter, 'This doctor is known as the butcher.'

Left alone in the waiting room, a prisoner in the chair, I looked through the window. The snow was white as the sheets on the hospital beds and probably just as cold, and it was overlaying itself with a thick blanket as the scurrying flakes tumbled from the greyness of a charcoal sky. The daylight was as uncertain as I was and the room reflected my gloom, as no lights could be switched on, even during daylight hours, without a blackout screen in position. I felt like blacking out.

'Lieutenant Richardson.' The soft voice beguiled me into a false sense of confidence. I obeyed the summons and submitted to the doctor. His face was red like unbled meat, florid yet jovial and it crowned a beefy body. In my mind his white coat became a blue and white butcher's apron and the stethoscope about his ears took on the ominous proportions of a humane killer. He played with a paper knife which looked large and keen enough to carve up a carcase. Mine felt to be already drained of blood. Anaesthetic, while not being readily available, was being sparingly used and because of wartime difficulties of supply was restricted to priority cases.

'There are disadvantages with anaesthetics. They make the patient feel sick and drowsy afterwards. You wouldn't like to miss today's sunshine, would you?' said the butcher prior to preparing to set a double fracture of the same bone.

The only sunshine was in my memory and that was being clouded over. I glanced outside. Noticing this the doctor said,

'Ah, well, it's like a picture postcard; too good to miss. I will set this without anaesthetic. It may be painful but only for a second and then it will all be over and you can count the snowflakes as they fall with a clear head and a cup of coffee.'

The X-ray plates were once more consulted as I was stretched upon the rack which was as cold as the benches outside. The doctor seemed to hesitate. He certainly hummed and ha-ed.

'Nurse, sit on his chest,' he said.

Like some all enveloping, gluttonous monster whose sadistic appetite was about to be satisfied, the seventeen stones of the fattest nurse that I ever seen descended upon me and, overflowing my ribcage obliterated the world beneath my chin. I fought for breath, gasping like a stricken haddock struggling for survival. My efforts to inflate my roller-flattened chest against this human Rock of Gibraltar were so painful that they cancelled out any sense of acute pain as my ankle was set in a couple of jerks.

'OK nurse; bring him back to the land of the living.'

The butcher looked human now, in fact, rather like a mother-figure, ample, warm, and caring and his stethoscope more like a baby's comforter. The human mountain heaved her mass from my chest like a slow, lumbering tank, daylight returned and I breathed again. A further X-ray proved that the doctor knew his job. Then my leg was encased in plaster from thigh to toe.

Deputy Fuhrer

'My undercarriage has been shot away,' came the startling signal, 'request permission to endeavour landing on flight deck or alternatively to ditch alongside.'

Lieutenant C.W. Scott spoke calmly and as clearly as if he had been asking permission to park a car. He had participated in an ariel attack on the toe of Italy.

'Prepare for crash landing on the flight deck. Emergency crews standby,' was the order which echoed through the tannoy system.

Executing a perfect circle the Swordfish turned astern of the aircraft carrier to attempt a landing. Gratefully the aircraft kissed the refuge of the deck by standing on her nose and wagging her tail in the air. Scottie's nose hit the instrument panel and part of his upper left jaw left its appointed position as it sought to peer from behind one eye. He eventually had an even worse fate for he found himself in the bed next to mine in Mearnskirk hospital.

We started a dynamic friendship which lasted until his death.

C.W. Scott was the renowned air pioneer who with Campbell-Black blazed the trail to Australia before the Second World War. The latter was killed in a flying accident over Blackpool, before the commencement of hostilities.

Scottie joined the Fleet Air Arm. He was a man of bright, ready humour but at the same time a very serious thinker. He professed atheism yet I am sure that his cheerful baiting was a cover for serious seeking. He would pick up the Bible beside my bed and, at first, treat it as if it was *Comic Cuts*. I was an engineer not an ordained man. Sister Jean Hodge, the night sister, was a well bred presbyterian, well versed in holy writ but in no way a theologian. Together we took on the formidable challenge from Scottie.

The hospital had been custom-built for children. The wards were delightful bright villas. The beds were child-length, the longest being five feet. As I am only five foot six inches the length of my bed did not cause me too much inconvenience but Scottie, a lean and lanky fellow, found himself each morning adding two feet, literally, to the overall dimensions of the bed. The Royal Navy had commandeered two adjacent wards, one for ratings and one for officers. A covered way bridged the hundred yards separating the two villas. The nursing staff were all trained for child care and had their pleasant routine shattered by the influx of mature and maimed mariners. We took advantage of the staff and made our own daily diet sheets. The solitary bath was three feet long, high sided and had remote control taps so that the children could not turn them on. It stood squarely in the middle of a very large bathroom. The only pieces of furniture in it were a cabinet for potties and an old harmonium. A naval officer suffering from signs of shellshock and receiving psychiatric treatment used to sooth his savaged breast by sitting for hours in the bathroom playing the only two tunes he knew; one was 'Abide with me' and the other wasn't. Whenever we required a bath we had to obtain a key to the taps from a nurse who invariably said either 'It's about time, too.' or 'Can I do you now, Sir?'

When I indulged in ablutions my plastered leg would not fit into the bath but pointed heavenward like a steeple in scaffold.

There were two officers of equal rank in our ward. Both were Welshmen and both were called W.H. Davies. One had sustained serious head wounds which required a trepanning operation which, when carried out, was filmed as the operation was delicate and unusual. During the operation he had lost a certain amount of blood. The other Davies had stomach trouble. The former was put on a supply of blood tablets while the other should have received moving potions.

'Davies is not showing progress, doctor. In fact he is deteriorating,' reported the staff nurse.

The doctor examined him.

'You know, doctor,' said the hesitant patient, 'I'm sure that I would get well quickly if you didn't pump all that cascara into me. I'm never off the bedpan.'

'It's not cascara, Davies,' the doctor's voice came through the patient's head bandages, 'it's blood.'

'It has the same effect.' said the desperate Davies.

The convoy of consultants eventually reached the bedside of the stomach sufferer.

'Can you give me anything to move my bowels? I feel that I am cemented up. What about a charge of dynamite?' suggested Davies who was a demolition officer.

Then the penny dropped. Treatment was adjusted to the correct patient and the wilting Welshman ceased to wilt while the other was greatly moved.

The day room was a bright, spacious place adorned with nursery rhymes and a rocking horse. Comfortable armchairs and a couple of writing desks had been placed in it for our use. A fireplace had been opened up and the warming glow of burning coals chased away the winter's gloom. The night time hours turned the day room into a quiet oasis of debate for Jean Hodge.

Scottie had ceased criticising or ridiculing the scriptures but sought, as an aeronaut, engineer and world traveller some assurance of the existence of God and of His Fatherhood. Jean and I joined forces.

'Where is the love of God in nature? Nature is one big battlefield of tooth and claw. Fish fights fish and bird fights bird, beast is against beast and man, as we see him today, is inhuman. In the whole history of man we find conflict and evil. How can He allow Hitler to keep on perpetrating his evil destruction upon innocent peoples? Where is there any evidence that there is a caring God? Man, you say, is made in the image of God. My God, what a God,' began Scottie's first broadside against the battlements of our belief.

Night after night, week after week, this trinity of amateur theologians battled on, locked in serious and continuing debate. Looking back I can see it was yet another step towards my commitment to the ministry.

It was stimulating; it was challenging. Jean was superb. I was in hospital for a period of eleven weeks and Scottie for ten. He surprised us in the last week of his incarceration by asking Jean to arrange his baptism. He had no interest in any denomination. He was simply a convinced Christian. Padre Young, a presbyterian, spent a couple of sessions with him and then baptized him with Jean and me standing as sponsors. At a special midnight baptism tea in the dayroom, the scene of our seminary, Jean cut the cake and Scottie gave her a gold cross on a chain. The following day we were sad to see him to leave us though pleased at his recovery. He had been admitted needing physical repairs and had left healed in body and spirit; or did he? Three days after his discharge he blew his brains out.

Adolf Schicklgrubber, alias Adolf Hitler, woke up one fine day to find that his bedfellow had absconded. The Deputy Fuhrer of the Third Reich had deserted the gang of cut throats. Rudolph Hess was no aeronaut but his acquired plane obeyed the laws of gravity and returned to earth among the heather and the haggis of Bonnie Scotland depositing its unconscious pilot into a five foot bed in Mearnskirk Hospital. He was carried in for he had emulated me and broken his ankle. He regarded himself as vice-captain of the Nazis in the league of desperadoes. Until his removal, within a week, he shared with us the joys and tribulations of the hospital. A Royal Marine guard armed with a bamboo cane in case any rash Hun should seek to retrieve their terrier, stood at the door of the little side room which was to be Hess's Fourth Reich for a short while but the door leading to a veranda was left unguarded.

Jenny was a Scots lass in plenty, for she was at least thirteen stones and only seventeen years of age. She was eternally cheerful and when she laughed she wobbled and when she stopped laughing she still wobbled. She was conscientious even though, as a probationer nurse, she was heavily committed to the bedpan routine. Nothing disturbed her happy way of life and in a nice way she didn't care a damn for anyone.

'I am shaving. Take that porridge away until I have finished. I will ring when I am ready,' thus ordered harassed, hungry Hess as he tackled his stubble and Jenny duly complied.

The bell rang.

'Hey, Jenny. Yon Hun is hungry,' punned the cook, 'Tak him his breakfast.'

Jenny entered the room. The patient sat up in bed. Jenny placed the porridge on the straddling bed table. Hess contemplated the mess of pottage before him and, as Jenny was about to leave the room, complained.

'This is the porridge you brought me half an hour ago.

Obviously it has been on a hot plate. Take it away and bring me fresh porridge.'

The tubby wee lass from the highlands, the probationer nurse, turned to the Deputy Fuhrer of the German Reich and said,

'You'll eat that up or go without. Don't you know there's a war on?'

I was sorry to see Hess leave. I watched with special interest the trial proceedings at Nuremburg and I feel that Hess should never have been incarcerated in Spandau Gaol for so long. To me it was inhuman and I feel that the Allies should have insisted that Russia agree to his release or released the old man unilaterally.

Dead March

The night was cold and eerie as the pale moon in an arctic sky cast a mystic pattern of darkness upon the frost-encrusted snow. The whole of nature seemed to be fair nithered as the temperature bottomed the thermometer. One man was driven to seek permanent exile from the outrageous extremities of northern weather by committing suicide.

'Wakey, wakey, you lot.'

The night sister emulated a master-at-arms and in good service tradition continued; 'volunteers please.'

Normally such a rude awakening would have sickened the average patient but this was especially horrific as the hour was midnight. Who but the nocturnal creatures who hunted in the night would wish to open their eyes at such an ungodly hour? We had all been obediently tucked up in our little children's beds while the bulk of the hospital staff cavorted in lancers, polkas and waltzes at their annual staff dance in Glasgow. They had left behind one nurse for each ward, one sister for the whole of the naval section and an on-duty doctor who couldn't go to the dance anyway as he was confined to his bed with influenza. Jean Hodge was at the dance so Scottie and I were in our narrow pits.

Roused from the dreams of the innocent and from the balm of soothing sleep the lights dazzled our resisting eyes.

'A naval doctor has just been brought in from a ship lying at Greenock,' the sister began to explain.

'He attempted suicide by injecting himself with a massive dose of morphine. Being a doctor he probably made a successful job of it and our task will probably be hopeless. Still, while there is life there is hope and we must try.'

'How can we help?' asked one of the patients.

'We must keep his circulation going. To do this I want him carried shoulder high up and down the corridor while we slap him with wet towels. It may be a long job and certainly exhausting but I feel that we ought to try,' was the reply.

'Come on, Jack, put your good leg forward,' said Scottie as he nearly broke my other leg as he heaved me from the bed.

'Well, I don't know what he can do with his wooden leg,' pondered the sister.

Laughing, I prepared to snuggle down again in my nice warm bed.

'Let's see,' the sister considered, 'Yes, you can sit at the wash basin in the bathroom and soak the towels for us. Come on everybody, lend a hand.'

Then in good naval fashion she yelled,

'Get fell in.'

There was no shortage of volunteers. A warrant officer, in with stomach trouble, had given himself shore leave and had returned slightly inebriated. He was a gunnery officer used to drilling recruits. As I positioned myself at the washbasin he took up station ahead of the body-carrying party. Four men carried the stricken doctor moving his legs and arms as they walked while nurses wielded the sodden towels to bash the doctor's bare torso. Nurses had been brought from the neighbouring children's ward. The warrant officer kept them all in time barking out,

'Left, right, left, right, turn to the right at the end; about turn!'

As long as he was happy no one rebuked him.

Individuals of the body-party weakened, stumbled and became exhausted so had to be relieved, so it was not long before I was transferred from the handbasin to the doctor's left arm. I thumped along, my plastered leg receiving unexpected therapy and sounding like long John Silver's peg leg. Instead of fifteen men on a dead man's chest it was a dead man on our chests, for we carried him long after he had ceased to breathe.

'Oh, I'm sorry' said a nurse as she clouted me into unconsciousness.

Her tired arm had affected her aim and her heavy wet towel landed like a load of bricks on the back of my neck. By then I was carrying the man's shoulder so there was already a list to port and as I fell the body tumbled also and the head hit the deck with a resounding but ominous crack.

The smile which had been constantly on the doctor's face seemed to be fixed as he stopped breathing. By now scarcely an inch of skin remained on the man for he had been constantly and conscientiously whipped with sodden towels for about five hours. The other bearers stopped and,

exhausted, found support from the walls or sat on the deck.
One nurse attended me while the sister examined the
medic. She held a mirror to his lips.

'Looks as if he's gone,' she said and then began to thump
on his chest as if trying to knock on the door of life. Then
she sent for the hospital doctor. He came from his sick bed,
still in his pyjamas. He adjusted his stethoscope, straddled
the body and fainted. Volunteers carried him into a side
room.

'Better carry him a little longer,' suggested the sister.

Once again a more subdued cortege resumed its march.

I was back at the sink wringing out the blood-soaked
towels when the sister decided that the man was beyond
earthly recall.

'Thank you, everybody. At least we tried. Back to bed.'

The dead doctor was conveyed to a room adjacent to that
of the sick doctor. Hospital routine for the dead began to
function. A queue formed at the bathroom. My nightdress
was badly stained with blood and I had to obtain a new one.
Because my plaster prevented the wearing of pyjamas I had
a regular supply of nighties upon which the more artistic of
the patients drew butterflies and daisies while the less
cultured inscribed doubtful slogans. While we waited to
wash or bath, the strains of 'Abide with me' peeled
solemnly in funeral tones from the harmonium.

'What happens now?' I queried of the sister, as she busily
laid out the body.

'We get him ready for the day porter to take the mortuary
and inform the naval authorities,' was her reply.

'What about a prayer?' I asked.

'Yes, I think that's a splendid idea. If you say one I will
come in with you.'

Together we knelt at the dead man's bedside. It seemed
as if all the world was holding its breath in reverence, for no
sound filtered through. It was a solemn moment and to me
most impressive. With pity and trying to understand I knelt
in silence. The biblical text, 'What purpose this waste?'
worried my mind. What had driven this young doctor to

take such a drastic action? Did he have a wife, children or living parents? One thing was certain, he was some mother's son. I prayed, little knowing that my faith was to be further challenged by the suicide of my dear friend Scottie.

After prayers my clean nightie and I snuggled down in bed. The winter's night had not yet yielded to the day when, like a clarion call, came the summons;

'Time to get up.'

We were back to normal.

Sobieski

Returning from sick leave I found myself in Glasgow standing in the naval headquarters and before a barnacled, old re-incarnation of Captain Bligh. There was no bounty in his manner nor did he call me Christian. Swiftly he perused my documents.

'Do you speak Polish?' he barked out.

'No, sir.'

'Then begin to learn to do so. You are due to join *Sobieski*' he informed me.

'When, sir?' I enquired.

'Straight away. She sails this afternoon from the Tail of the Bank. You are on light duties for two months,' Barnacle Bill informed me without even looking at me.

'What have I to do on the ship, Sir?' I asked.

'Interpret.'

I knew nothing about Poland except that she appeared to be the reason that we were at war. Years back, I could recall, my history master told me about Bonny Prince Charlie but I had been more interested in Flora McDonald than in remembering that somewhere in Charlie's name was Sobieski. Limping into the drafting office I learnt that *Sobieski* was still in King George Vth dock.

The taxi dropped me alongside and I went on board. Nick, a Pole, was the purser who spoke English with a good Geordie accent. He seemed to be the first person I had met that day who knew everything about me. He and I became firm friends and from him I found out that the entire crew had endured the worst Nazi-Germany could hurl at them; torture, incarceration, family slaughter and untold hardships. All had somehow escaped to serve with the Free Polish Forces. The captain was the only man who was not a Pole. He was an Austrian, an ardent anti-Nazi from the early days of Hitler's rise to power and an ex U-boat commander of the First World War, and an admirer of Pastor Martin Niemoeller. He spoke excellent, though clipped, English. He assured me that his ship was safe, simply because he knew how German submariners thought. What he didn't know was how the German Luftwaffe pilots thought, for that very first night, our sailing having been delayed, the Germans launched a vicious air attack on Glasgow.

My cabin was too warm. The Poles insisted on having the accommodation heating turned up to the absolute. So I was absolutely perspiring as I lay in my sumptuous bunk. To offset the hellish heat I wore no nightclothes and even spurned the shame-covering sheet. The heat was oppressive but beyond my control.

Suddenly the vessel rocked alarmingly. The heat of my cabin was now accentuated by all Hell being unleashed outside. A stick of bombs straddled the dock and in a twinkling fires were raging around us. Sirens began to wail as the infamous Glasgow blitz began.

Nick rushed into my cabin.

'Grab your helmet and join me on the bridge,' he breathlessly shouted.

He and I had an action station at an oerlikon gun on the port wing of the bridge. I raced up there to see fire and fury being unleashed all around us. The Poles slung all they had at the German planes above. Soon I was in team with Nick firing desperately and wildly into the vastness of an alien sky. Starshells mingled with searchlights, and bomb blasts with the raging fires ashore. Bells rang as bullets screamed. One thousand people were to die before the all-clear sounded. A nearby warehouse showered us with burning debris as it disintegrated into wreckage. The momentum of the conflict and the imperative demands of concentration were so acute that it was not for a space of over ten minutes that I realized that apart from my tin helmet I was completely starkers. That sight alone should have startled the Luftwaffe away. Long after the all-clear was sounded and shore batteries and ships had ceased firing *Sobieski's* guns were still blazing. So intent were they that they fired at anything and everything, even shooting-stars.

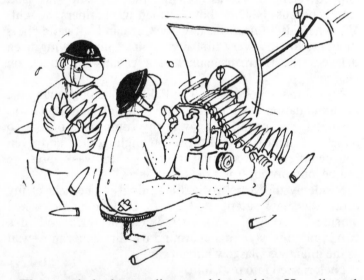

The captain had a peculiar, revolting hobby. He collected every kind of weird wicked, but to him wonderful, bug, insect or creepy creature. One wall of his cabin held glass show-cases which were full of pin ups, tarantulas, scorpions, wood wasps and the like, all happily, from my point of view, chloroformed and despatched.

One afternoon while in the Atlantic I joined the captain at

his table for tea. He relished the horror on my face when I saw, dominating the table, an inverted pickle jar containing the most evil looking creature that I have ever seen. This massively proportioned, spider-like thing seemed to have innumerable eyes which gazed in all directions at the same time.

'The cook found it in a crate of bananas we've just cracked open. Isn't it a beauty?' the captain enthused.

The thing was positively wicked and ugly.

'Steward,' ordered the captain, 'go to the galley and bring me some cockroaches.'

The steward, expressing no surprise and evidently accustomed to such orders, produced a goodly supply of these unfortunate bait.

They were delivered as unwilling gladiators into the pickle jar. With a frightening speed the creature captured and devoured the cockroaches as they vainly endeavoured to scale the glass walls of their condemned cell.

The captain lifted the jar from his Frankenstein horror. It seemed to fix its evil eyes towards me as I beat a very hasty retreat.

Later that night I was reluctant to accept the captain's invitation to his cabin for drinks, but was greatly heartened when I saw evil-eyes duly pinned and labelled, with its unpronounceable name entered into the captain's Book of Remembrance.

Nick, the purser, had suffered under the cruel regime of the Nazi occupation of Poland and in common with most of us longed to have Hitler's name in a 'Book of Remembrance'.

Nick had been arrested at his home in Cracow while eating his breakfast. His crime was that he was the borough treasurer and a non-collaborator with the German overlords. His wife was taken away at the same arrest and he never saw her again. For weeks he was kept, not in a concentration camp, but in an overcrowded prison cell. One morning the cell door was clanked open and all the inmates ushered out into the sweetness of the crisp, morning air and the bitterness of Nazi inhumanity. They were joined by other captives and together were marched to a railway siding. An engine, already at full steam, was coupled to a long line of cattle trucks and into each truck was loaded about eighty human beings of all ages and both sexes. It was twelve hours before the engine began to haul its grim load towards death and another distant siding. There the engine was uncoupled but the doors of the trucks were not opened for almost another three weeks. Four people survived from Nick's truck. He had kept alive by licking the condensation from the small glass windows near the roof of the truck. He wept as he recalled to me the unspeakable privations, the insanity and the stench of death and the tortured actions of his dying compatriots. Though terribly disturbed mentally, as well as physically, he was again imprisoned. For months he languished in another gaol only to learn that yet another railway journey awaited him. He escaped and after eight months of Continental wanderings with suffering, hardship, fear and injury as his companions, he arrived in Harwich. Yet, amazingly, he held no bitterness despite the iron that had entered into his soul. He had a simple trust in God and in the ultimate triumph of God's love even though it seemed as if the Satanic powers of evil were then invincible. He longed for the re-establishment of peace and security in the land he loved so much. He told me his stories of inhumanity in such a manner that he appeared to be apologetic for those Germans who debased human dignity and decency in carrying out the commands of their power-crazed, evil superiors.

The grey dangers of the Atlantic's dawns and dusks seemed to stimulate a challenge to our skipper. Like a stalking lynx with power, speed and unexcelled cunning he would leave our appointed station with the convoy to seek and destroy U-boats rather than wait for them to attack.

'I know how they think. I know how they work. I know when it is likely to expect an attack because I was one of

74

them and I can still think like them and so anticipate them.'

His hunting instincts and frequent excursions from the convoy screen as he tally-hoed after the quarry frequently occasioned me to answer frantic signals from the convoy commodore who on one occasion signalled 'Quo vadis?' and another, a plaintive 'Please do not come back.' I came to understand the pidgin-English of our captain and crew and also their frustrations and tensions.

While in the Clyde I heard a fearful commotion in the starboard passage outside my cabin door. Dashing out I was to witness a seaman in the act of plunging a knife into the side of one of his shipmates. He had beaten him down to the deck and, pinning him there, tried to stab the unfortunate underdog in his chest. With a desperate twist the seaman saved his life at the expense of his side which now began to pour out blood. Almost immediately the assailant became the saviour as he tried to stem the flow of blood and to comfort the other man.

'Why did he do it, Nick?' I asked the purser.

'A woman, of course, and a prostitute at that.' he answered.

'It doesn't seem to me to be a good enough reason for a murderous attack,' I replied.

'Understand this. These men have been forcibly separated from their families. Some don't know if their families are still alive. They needed an outlet. This lad had found one in a prostitute. He became so involved with her that he grew to love her and regard her as his exclusive property. She was his. She was all he had apart from his shipmates and his hopes. Last night his special friend on board came back from a run ashore and spoke enthusiastically of the hour he had spent with a prostitute.

"Wow, what a girl. Did she know her stuff. Never had one like her."

'Elaborating on the past-time it became clear to the listener that his shipmate, his own particular friend, had been with his lady of the lamplight. Enraged, he attacked his friend who fled along the passage only to be caught outside your cabin. The rest you know,' concluded Nick.

'What happened to him?' I queried, 'Who will deal with him?'

'Oh, it's all hushed up. The two men are friends again and the stab wound was not serious. The girl has lost a good supply of chocolate, smokes and soap. By the way, as you always eat at the captain's table, don't mention it to him. He knows nothing about it,' advised Nick.

I rather suspected that the captain did know but was too good a sailor and diplomat to do anything about it.

Too soon my duties on board *Sobieski* came to an end, and after weeks of Atlantic adventures she sailed without me down the evening waters of the Clyde. I experienced a personal bereavement when I heard that she had been torpedoed and sunk with all hands in the Mediterranean.

For almost forty years I felt that sorrow until the day the insurance man called upon me at Mitford Vicarage. I had known Bill Gilholme for over sixteen years and now for the first time he spoke to me of his being seasick.

'I was on my way back from the Far East, after the war was over. The Indian Ocean made my stomach somersault and the seascape green. I wished I could die.'

'What ship?', I asked.

'*Sobieski*.' was his astonishing reply.

He confirmed his story later by bringing to me a photograph dated 1946.

She had survived. God bless her and all who sailed in her.

So, looking back down the aisles of time which led me once again to those treacherous wartime days, I felt again the fellowship, dedication and loyalty that made golden the sunset as *Sobieski*, silhouetted against a westering sky sailed down the Clyde and I returned north to Inveraray.

Royal Descent

Lord Louis Mountbatten fresh from his epic in HMS

Kelly succeeded Lord Roger Keyes as head of Combined Operations. Lord Louis' coming to Inveraray, where so many thousands of sailors and soldiers were trained, housed and shipped, lifted the sagging morale of the training-stale personnel.

He came; he saw; he conquered the confidence and spirit of the men.

There was, however, a large contingent of wrens, so it wasn't very long afterwards that Princess Marina, Duchess of Kent, came to Inveraray. I was involved in this way.

Our ship had been out in the grey waters of the North Sea for a lengthy period and it was with relief and also joy that we saw on either side of us in the mists of morning light the shores of Loch Fyne. The hills around the loch failed to emerge clearly this morning, for the clouds hung low to disclose the source of the fountain of torrential rain. The waters of the loch and the sky were united in one huge wetness. Despite a morning that mourned we were pleased to be in those waters. Reaching terra firma I found the weed covered rungs of an iron ladder which threatened to dissolve into the wet morass of the skeleton which served as a jetty.

I was very tired for I had been on duty in the middle watch and it was nine o'clock in the morning when our ship found its buoy. Clad in a sou'wester, oilskin and seaboots I was as yet unshaven and wearing a towel about my neck to prevent the rain from soaking my midriff. I walked up what should have been dry land to the admin. offices of the Combined Operations headquarters of HMS *Quebec*.

It was good to feel land under my feet even though it hid under a stream of rain.

My heart and my mind were set on the hope that there would be mail in the headquarters for me and for my ship's company.

Squelching steadfastly and steeply and still in a semi-stupor of sleep, I was rudely shattered, not only by the driving rain but the earth-shattering voice of Commander Cassidy.

'Jack, just the man I want,' he shouted.

'Why? What have I done?' I gurgled through the storm.

'Princess Marina is coming here to open the Wrens' new sick bay and to inspect the girls.'

'Oh, that's grand,' I replied with eager enthusiasm. 'When?'

'This forenoon. All our rehearsals have been outdoors and just look at the bloody weather,' complained the worthy commander.

He gave further blasphemous opinions of the allegedly illegitimate rain.

After his torrent of abuse he came to the point.

'We've moved everything into the boatshed. See, those high rails will prevent the official car from getting alongside.'

The high rails were used to haul the landing craft for 'dry-docking'.

'So I want you to escort Princess Marina the 100 yards or so from her car to the boat shed under cover of an umbrella,' he explained.

'What's wrong with all these subbies?' I asked.

'They'd probably fall over themselves. No. I want you.' emphasized the commander.

Feeling greatly honoured, I agreed.

'I'd love to; in fact it would be a change and a privilege. I'll just go back on board after I've collected the ship's mail, get washed, have a shave and get shifted into a decent rig.'

'Like Hell you will.' protested my superior, 'The princess is due here in ten minutes. You'll find a golf umbrella in my cabin. See you down here,' and off he sped to demoralize and devastate the junior officers.

The gamp was huge and multi-coloured. I took up position in the doorway of the main boathouse. Behind me a very young and new sub-lieutenant, R.N.V.R. shivered in his gunnery gaiters as they glittered upon his nervous legs.

A double row of rifle-kitted seamen waited at ease and lots of Wrens had stopped their flight to stand in dragooned array about the dampening deck of the depository for damaged landing craft.

'Excuse me, sir,' spoke the gunnery officer to me, 'from where I'm standing I won't be able to see when the royal car arrives. Could you give me a signal when it's here?'

'Certainly, I'll do that,' then trying to calm his obvious nervous syndrome I remarked, 'and may I say that you look very smart. I'm sure that the princess will be very impressed.'

'It's not the princess I'm worried about; it's the commander.'

'Oh, don't worry about him. He's alright really; his bark is much worse than his bite,' I consoled.

In fact the car was one hour adrift of schedule. As the waiting moments were counted by pelting raindrops the gunnery officer became more and more nervous and my right ear itched.

I rubbed it. Immediately the pregnant silence was hastened to a premature climax as the order was barked out.

'Guard... Royal salute... P R E S E N T... A R M S !'

The bugler dutifully sounded the alert which resembled something like Handel's 'Water Music'.

There was nothing watery about the commander's vocabulary. After doubting the legitimacy of the gunnery officer's parenthood, the boss demanded an explanation.

'Sir, Lieutenant Richardson gave me the sign,' he protested and shifted the buck on to me.

'Oh no,' I asserted, 'my ear was itching.'

The rain continued its rhythmic beat upon the roof, the morning light dimmed its wick, the commander muttered under his breath about the goodness of God and the gunnery officer wished that the flood would overwhelm us all. The boatshed resembled Noah's Ark when suddenly it seemed the waters divided and the hour was fulfilled.

With my imperial gamp at full hoist and accompanied by two Wrens I ran to the car. One Wren was to open the car door and the other to curtsey.

I placed my protective parasol in perfect position, one Wren opened the car door and the other Wren fainted.

Princess Marina, resplendent in her Commodore's uniform, was too advanced in the process of getting out of the car to avoid stepping lightly on the Wren's neck as the girl lay prostrate in the mud.

What a propaganda picture it would have proved if some Nazi photographer had been able to secure it!

After the princess had helped the Wren and comforted her, and the ulcers in the commander's innards perilously popped, I navigated the princess over the troubled waters into the haven where she would be. Eventually she sallied forth to be driven to the mile-distant, new sick bay. My gamp gambol graciously gained a lee-side gangway for Marina back to her car. Off it sped over the unmade and unfathomable road to the sick bay.

'Double up behind them,' yelled the commander at me.

So I ran, seaboots heavy below the Plimsoll line and a multi-coloured umbrella like a marker buoy upon an uncharted sea, behind the royal car which soon out-distanced me. When I reached the sick bay the princess had completed her inspection. She said sweet things to me, I think, but my waterlogged lugs made words unintelligible. Anyway, not even the rain could obliterate the rainbow of Princess Marina's smile for me. If she had kissed me I would have willingly turned into a toad!

One thing the princess didn't know. She was to open the new sick bay for Wrens but in Inveraray where all the bugs, viruses and germs were either drowned or attuned only to marine life, there was no sickness. So at 0900 the Wrens were paraded and a dozen were detailed to report to the sick bay with nighties at the ready. When they were tucked into their little pits, the doctor carefully distributed ill-health among them, taking care that none had anything that was infectious. After Princess Marina had walked among them and commiserated at their misfortunes they were told to report back for normal duties. I went back on board with the mail and a good story, and had a shave – just in case.

The gracious and well-loved royal lady was soon followed to Inveraray by someone the whole nation and Commonwealth not only respected but loved; our King George VI.

As he stepped from the jetty to the R-boat he very courteously and humbly asked the coxswain, who was an able seaman, if he may take the wheel and he brought the boat alongside our ship expertly.

He clambered on board, went round the ship with as little fuss as possible, showed great interest in the different departments connected with Combined Operations, spoke to all and sundry and finally ended up in the wardroom for tea.

It was a simple tea and didn't last long and eventually the King relaxed, leaned back in his chair and lit a cigarette. He had hardly done this when an aide informed him that he was now due to go up on the upper deck. He took a lingering look at the cigarette, had another puff, reached for his cap and went up top, the cigarette concealed in his left hand.

He saw that all the ship's company were manning ship to cheer him goodbye. He nipped the lighted end of the cigarette and dropped the stub carefully into the scupper, walked to the gangway, saluted us and was soon once again at the wheel of the R-boat.

No sooner had he left the ship than there was a concerted rush to the scupper to retrieve the cigarette butt dropped by His Majesty. That night the fag-end was lighted again and passed round quickly to all the sailors who had one draw, passed it on, another puff and passed it on, and as many as wanted smoked it until there was only one tattered dog-end of a fag left, almost too small to smoke. So the sailors decided to raffle it in aid of the Red Cross. I was asked to conduct the selling of tickets and we made a profit of £84 for the Red Cross.

The seaman who won the fag-end preserved it all the time he was on our ship and I should imagine that even today this tattered cigarette lies proudly in someone's china cabinet.

Shoresides

The southbound train rumbled through the night. The darkness outside was intensified by the absence of a moon and the enforced black-out. Within the first-class carriage one, solitary, blue-tinted lightbulb failed to give substance to the seats of the passengers who occupied them. Only one traveller was not in uniform. She was an elderly lady who, removing her spectacles, began to knit mechanically.

'Comforts for the troops,' she explained.

Her needles clicked in time with the carriage wheels as they subdued the lengths of rails. She could not see to knit, neither could I distinguish the colour of the wool or whether she was knitting a balaclava, a sweater or a pair of seaboot stockings. In that light it could turn our to be either or all.

I could not see to read so I shut my eyes and let my memories illuminate me.

Robbie and Mac had come to Glasgow to bid me farewell. Parting is such sweet sorrow but Shakespeare could never have experienced the bitter sweetness of this parting, for I had no desire to be going. My departure had been decreed by my lords at the Admiralty. I was drafted to a shore job and hated the idea but had to report to the Admiralty in Whitehall.

Resplendent in my smartest uniform recently purchased at Johnnie Geives with my approaching marriage in mind, I waited in the foyer of the Station Hotel for my two shipmates. A tweed clad, school-marm figure approached me.

'Porter, take my bags to my room. Here's the key.'

She addressed me. The key was fastened to a tally large enough to secure a battleship and indicated that her room was on the third floor.

'Certainly, madam,' I replied.

With the correct degree of servility I began to struggle with two large and unwieldy suitcases, two smaller ones and an umbrella.

'One moment, young man,' she deterred me.

She spoke as if to an erring student and then vanished out of sight to return dragging behind her a rather reluctant hound usually connected with sausages eaten by the enemy. She handed the dog lead to me and I was amazed at the dexterity of my efforts to control my burdens. I found her room, placed the bags, mistress and pooch within it and was withdrawing again when she demanded my attention. She opened her purse, fumbled intently among the notes and produced a silver threepenny piece with which she rewarded me.

'Have room service send me up a cup of tea,' was her final

request.

I removed my naval cap, gave a little bow, thanked her for her patronage and respectfully retired backwards.

I arranged with reception to have her tea sent to her together with my card.

A further indignity followed. Robbie was well over six feet tall and had a horror of becoming round shouldered, so he spoke to people while keeping his head upright and without inclination. This gave him the unintentional air of superiority and he could have been, unjustly, dubbed a snob. Although always on his dignity he was warm-hearted and genuine. The nickname given to him at Inveraray was 'Haw Haw'.

He and Mac boarded the bus with me. I went first, followed by Malcolm McCulloch while Robbie came up astern.

'Standing room only; no room upstairs. Pass along the bus, please,' restricted Robbie to the bus platform.

We pulled up at a bus stop and a dear old lady struggled aboard. Robbie helped her and as she squeezed into the interior she pressed two coins into Robbie's hand and said,

'A tuppenny one please.'

War

The blue light in the carriage gave me the blues as I continued with my recollections.

I had been part of the ship's company of HMS *Hydra*. She was a Combined Operations ship and a very happy one. The stewards had been incited to desert by a known Glasgow 'red'. The stewards were of the merchant navy on special wartime engagement with the Royal Navy. We watched them as they circled the ship in a cutter. Imagining that they were engaged in an abandon-ship exercise we hurled dubious advice to them and laughed heartily at their pathetic efforts with the oars which cut the air like uncertain windmills.

'Where are all the stewards?' the gunnery officer asked at teatime.

He had guts of gourmet proportions and was always prominent at meal times.

'There is nothing prepared. Where's the teapot? Sub, bring the chief steward to me,' he continued.

The young sub-lieutenant returned from a fruitless search which suggested an impending famine.

'I cannot find anyone, sir,'

Mac put forth the tentative suggestion.

'Probably they are all flaked out after their boat drill this afternoon, or they may even be marooned.'

'Boat drill?' queried the supply officer, 'They had no boat drill today.'

'Oh yes they did. We saw them at it' chorused the wardroom.

At dinner time there was no sign of food or stewards. This indeed was calamity.

'The shortest way to a man's heart is through his stomach' state the less romantic, but a cessation of victuals to that particular organ certainly activates the blood pressure and counter measures. A signal was sent ashore. Darkness and hunger fell around us. Three miles down the loch the blistered, weary stewards were espied sitting forlornly on the rock upon which their frail craft had foundered.

'Let them shiver until the morning,' ordered the commander from ashore.

It was my landing craft that was detailed to bring them back. They were repentant and chastised but were relieved that same day by a new batch of Royal Naval stewards.

Happy thoughts, but the snorting train tackled Beattock and took me further away from ships, assault craft and my special shipmates.

The Admiralty sent me to Woolwich and the Arsenal sent me to Crayford in Kent where I was appointed Assistant Gun Mounting Overseer. Our task was to oversee the manufacture of high angle/low angle gunnery directors and to accept them from Vickers on behalf of the Admiralty. I did not like to work. I missed the tang of the sea, the special atmosphere of shipboard life and the companions with whom I had shared fun and danger. For the sake of the war effort I tried to whip up enthusiasm, but factory floors and rolling platforms were not an inspiration. My immediate boss was lieutenant commander T.W.E. Dommett, affectionately known as 'Dammit'. He was a good man, helpful, considerate and efficient. The rest of the staff were all civilians.

Dammit rented a cottage in Kent. It had an old world attraction from the outside but I experienced an uncanny air about the inside. The living room was pleasant but an alcove from that room was definitely sepulchral and resisted the intrusion of daylight into its seclusion. It lent credence to the tale that the owner of the cottage used to sit in there for hours discussing affairs with her dead husband, such as the shape and inscription of his tombstone. The bookcase, hidden in the dark shadows, was full of tomes about tombs, spirits, seances and the occult of witchcraft.

One of Dammit's old shipmates was in the vicinity so the commander invited him to stay at the cottage. Together they had a 'run-ashore' in London and were returning, rather inebriated, through the village at two o'clock in the morning.

'You play the organ, don't you?' asked Dammit of his

friend.

'Yes,' came the reply, 'but I havn't done so for quite a while.'

'Well here's your chance,' tempted Dammit as they drew up alongside the village church.

They entered the dark and hallowed precincts and groped their stumbling way towards the organ which had been due for a refit since the time of the Battle of Trafalgar. It was locked. No light filtered through the stained glass windows and they were sufficiently aware that they could not break the black-out.

They took two candles from the sanctuary and in that dim light forced the organ lock with a pen knife.

The verger thought at first that the air-raid sirens were sounding, striding into the slumbers of the just, until his full consciousness revived. Then pulling a threadbare coat about his withered frame to supplement the thinness of his striped pyjamas, he betook himself to the church through sentinel angels and table tombs. The creaking of the old oak door was lost as the air was rent by the unsolemn lilting of the gasping organ. He fled to the vicarage.

The vicar was over eighty years of age and had recently contributed to the war effort by becoming a father.

'The devil is in the church and he's playing the organ,' panted the equally ancient verger as he verified his vision, 'I've seen him with my own eyes. Oh, it's horrible, vicar, horrible. It's Hell having its hour.'

Shrouding his clerical cloak over his flannelette nightshirt the vicar stealthily set off to assail the satanic powers. Despite the fact that he had scarcely enough breath on Sundays to read the lessons and had barely recovered from the shock of becoming a parent, he hastened through the darkened bushes and dampening grass to the church, aided no doubt by Michael and his heavenly host. He peered through the door. In the pale restricted light of the flickering candles he saw the nocturnal musicians as the notes of a bawdy sea-shanty shattered the solemnity of the vaulted timbers. Stone effigies, wooden cherubs and the vicar frowned their disapproval but the latter withdrew silently to the sanctity of his own bed. As he placed his cold, leathery feet against the warm softness of his young wife, he smiled.

The sizzling of the bacon in the frying pan seemed to blast the sensitive nerves of the two men as they sat at breakfast shielding their eyes from daylight, but Dammit's wife's voice avalanched as she said poetically,

'Tom, the vicar's here.'

The feeble form of the incumbent bent against the lintel of the door, for he had spent a disturbed night, yet to the men he was the judge and executioner rolled into one. The day of reckoning had arrived early, yet no condemnation was uttered.

'I was just passing on my way to say prayers at school assembly and thought that I would pop in as I have been told that you have a visitor,' guilessly intoned the cleric.

'How nice of you,' said Mrs Dammit, 'would you care for a coffee?'

'No, thank you; I must be about my business. Mind you I could have done with a stiff brandy this morning. During the night vandals broke into the organ and disturbed the Vicarage playing hymns that are not Ancient and Modern.'

'Oh dear,' said the commander's wife as the two men seemed to have been struck dumb. 'Was there much damage?'

'A little on the organ and a rather greasy mess of candle grease. Nothing that fifty pounds wouldn't put right. I thought that perhaps the commander might like to make a donation towards to cost of repairs.'

Then directing his attention towards Dammit himself the vicar continued,

'Your friend, too, no doubt, can play the organ.'

Dammit gulped; his visitor choked. The vicar placed a cheque for fifty pounds deep into the folds of his cassock pocket. He was smiling as he waved to them the following week from his new cycle.

Ethel signed on as my life shipmate. We began our voyage on the sea of matrimony at the thirteenth century parish church at Ryton-on-Tyne. Due to war shortages confetti was unobtainable but a bus inspector, who was also an amateur photographer tempted us to employ him in return for an ample supply of bus ticket clippings.

It was a showery day in April. Newcastle were playing away in a regional league.

The bus clippings were impregnated by the dampness and came at us like lumps of unstirred porridge. The photographs resembled a set-up in the chamber of horrors.

We set up home at Bexley, Kent. It was a most pleasant house with a bath at the bottom of the garden. It had been there for two thousand years testifying to the hygienic ablutions of the Romans. Utilizing the bend in the River Cray the Romans had employed the ingenious system of sluice gates which, when one end was opened, allowed their short canal to fill up. When they wanted to pull the plug they simply closed the one and opened the other. It saved on the water rate but we were involved with chest-deep watercress at every ablution.

We had another bathroom upstairs not nearly so inspiring. I was shaving before a small mirror which was fastened to the central wooden stanchion of the window frame, when I heard a knocking on the wall outside, yet I was upstairs!

A German fighter pilot had come out of the morning mist to machine-gun schoolgirls going to their lessons. Afterwards I found a bullet embedded in the window stanchion behind the mirror.

I liked Bexley. The vicar was mentally senile and so unable to fulfil his duties. He had been a naval chaplain and was with *Camperdown* when she sank at the end of the last century while executing a grid-iron manoeuvre. He asked me if I was there! Unable at first to get a replacement for him I was asked to help out even though I was an engineer. I was asked to look after the little mission of St.Barnabas on Dartford Heath. I had to preach. My knees knocked, my teeth gnashed, my spirit groaned within me as I wound my way to the pulpit. It was on the same floor level as the chancel and was octagonal. I couldn't find the door. I pushed every side without gaining access and finally climbed in only to fall out again as I leaned on the door which opened outward. A temporary incumbent was appointed and he lodged with us at Bath Cottage. He was an outstanding preacher as most Welshmen are. While he was resident with us his wife, in Wales, gave birth to a son who became the chairman of the Conservative Party, Mr. John Selwyn Gummer.

I did not really enjoy my work but rather endured it until, to my delight, I was drafted to Liverpool docks as assistant Fitting Out Gun Mounting Overseer.

At least I would be among ships.

A Question of Sin

Lieutenant Commander MacDonald was the original Ancient Mariner. He had sailed the seven seas in every kind of craft. He yarned of gunboats up the Yangtse River, of ice-breakers in Alaska and heart-breakers in Brazil. His favourite recollection was of being up the Nile in some shallow draught vessel when a seaman slipped overboard and came back on board minus a necessary part of equipment, his right leg, which they watched being devoured by a crocodile which no doubt found it, like Mac's stories, tough, salty and hard to digest.

Mac was my immediate superior at F.O.G.M.O. but we were both subordinate to a barnacled old engineer admiral who had been recalled for the duration.

This primate had one great gift. He could knit. Unfortunately he had not learnt how to execute corners or bends with his flailing needles, so he knitted scarves; long scarves for he didn't know how to stop and he gave them to us as comforts.

We had a staff of mainly ordnance artificers and seamen. We were responsible for the care and maintenance of gun mountings fitted on merchant ships and troop carriers. I was also divisional officer for the department.

Tug Wilson was one of my seamen ratings. He was universally disliked. He was a good workman but in every other way a devotee of the seven deadly sins, plus the two cardinal vices of maritime life; dirt and dishonesty. He was everything that one ought not to be in behaviour, speech, appearance and ambition. He was lower than Eden's serpent. Despite having a good wife and family he spent most of his leisure time explaining the Tree of Knowledge to a multitude of Eves; individually of course. He went home on leave and died. He told us about it AFTERWARDS.

Probably because of lying in so many strange beds or sweating with energetic Rahabs he contracted pneumonia when he reached home. He did not survive the crisis. He told me how he become conscious of looking at a body lying on a bed and recognising it as his own. Doctors were working frantically at it.

'I saw them thumping my chest, yet I felt detached. Then my bedside was obliterated by a thick, warm, comforting mist.'

Tug paused, thought seriously, as if recollecting something he could never forget.

'I felt that I was rising and experienced an overwhelming desire to part the mist and look beyond it.'

Then in deliberate, slow words he emphasized his belief.

'I am certain, absolutely convinced, that through the mist lay light and beauty and joy in such quality that it exceeded anything on this earth.'

Again he paused.

'Don't ask me how I know this, why I should be so convinced that there was life and a life to be desired beyond the mist. I felt it so strongly that it must be real.'

Then Tug continued.

'I willed myself desperately to pass through but felt the

imposition of weightfulness on my shoulders. I began to ache. The mist was above me as I seemed to be falling. Strangely I felt a burning sensation beneath my eyebrows. The pain returned. I opened my eyes and saw a doctor, I reckon that I died.'

This was confirmed to him when a week later his doctor told him that he had been considered as dead for almost three minutes.

This experience must have been real for it had a tremendous, reforming effect on Tug. After an extension of leave he returned to us a completely changed man. He now earnestly endeavoured to please, to re-direct his steps and to guard his language. He kept himself clean and honest for he declared that he did not wish by any wrong deed to forfeit that upon whose threshold he had stood.

Stripey was the opposite. He was religious, fervently so, with his bible in his shirt pocket and a biblical quotation for every phase or incident. He was a member of the Select Brethren. Prayers, not blasphemy, were the fruit of his lips and his concern for his fellow workers was shown in his many warnings of spiritual pitfalls administered to officers and ratings alike.

We were all housed in the Liver Building, room 222 on the second floor. Returning one morning from an early inspection of a troop carrier I found an elderly woman sitting in my outer office. She was shabbily dressed. Her face without any make-up was rather repulsive and bumping down its wrinkles tears ran an obstacle course. She appeared to be over sixty years of age and looked forlorn and sad.

'Good morning. Can I help you?' I asked.

The only response was an increase in the tempo of the sobbing. Greatly concerned, I put my arm around her shoulders and gently led her from the hard wooden bench on which she had been sitting to the comfort of an easy chair in my office.

'Stripey', I called.

'Yes sir' came the answer from over the dividing wall.

'Come here, please. I need you.'

This gnarled, old grandfather and Plymouth Brother came into my office like a tidal wave. His glance was directed at the old woman.

'Make her a cup of tea, Stripey. Do you take sugar and milk?'

To my surprise it was Stripey who answered.

'Only milk, sir; no sugar.'

He departed to the heads, as we term the lavatories in the navy, to fill the kettle.

My phone rang, and I am sure that Mac could hear the sobs of the woman which punctuated every word I spoke.

'Jack, can you come around. I've got some rabbits.' asked Mac.

Rabbits in the navy are certain items, desirable or hard to obtain items, which have probably been acquired in a dubious manner, in other words, underhand.

In wartime there were lots of them such as oranges, tins of meat or chocolate which the men used to 'obtain' from the ships.

'Sorry Mac. I'm tied up at the present. I'll be along afterwards.'

The high tide of tears continued to flow. Stripey seemed to be taking his time with the kettle. The pathetic figure never lifted her eyes until he returned with the tea. She slopped it into her saucer and finally Stripey took it from her.

'Has she told you, sir?'

'Not a word. Let her get pulled together. Is your tea to your liking? Care for a biscuit?'

Again it was the seaman who answered.

'She doesn't eat sweet biscuits, sir, but she'll be alright. Won't you?'

At last a sign of response.

Through her tears she gurgled a grunt and lifted her clouded eyes towards Stripey like a pleading spaniel or a stranded cod.

'Has she told you, sir?' queried Barnacle Bill a second

time, 'I mean, has she said anything?'

I began to admire Stripey for he displayed an apparently genuine concern and seemed to be able to communicate far better than I could. I seemed to be getting nowhere and I was mentally commending Stripey for his spiritual administration of comfort and understanding. How naive I was regarding his Christian and Good Samaritan efforts.

When I replied in the negative he answered with this request.

'Can you find her accommodation for a few days until I can get her fixed up? Anything will do; one room or the Salvation Army hostel.'

'Is she homeless?'

'In a way sir,' was Stripey's reply.

She still sat mute although her sobs had subsided but she offered no contribution to the two-man conversation. For a while Stripey never spoke and I waited for the woman to speak.

Finally, Stripey's unprofaned lips moved.

'You see, sir, her husband came home early from night shift and caught her in bed...with me.'

I looked at the old woman who now resembled a sodden piece of knotted string and then at Stripey whose corrugated face remained impassive and for a moment I wondered what it would be like for anyone to see those two heads together on a pillow.

'What happened?'

'Oh, nothing, sir. We just slept together for company,' replied Stripey.

'I didn't mean that, nor do I believe you. I meant, what happened when her husband caught you both?' I said.

'Well, sir, he threw us both out. I had to knock again at the door for my clothes. He let us both in to dress and told her never to come back again.'

'Has she any family?' I asked.

'All married and away. She's a lonely woman. I was just trying to help her,' pleaded the seamen.

Instead of finding her accommodation I took her home

and effected, with difficulty, a reconciliation. I felt sorry for her husband for he was really past the age for working nightshifts but it was his war effort.

When I left them she was changing the bedsheets and I assured the man that I would speak strongly to the erring sailor.

'Aren't you rather a hypocrite, Stripey? A pillar of your community sharing a pillow with Rahab.' I asked.

'Oh no, sir,' came the prompt reply from a rather hurt brother 'Definitely not. You see, a sin is only a sin if one regards it as a sin. I don't think that I sinned.' Theology. Contemporary perhaps, convenient certainly.

One of my most respected colleagues on F.O.G.M.O. staff was David Minto.

Born in South Shields, he lived in America and was an elocutionist to the Metro-Mayer Film Studios. He taught several of the world's best known stars how to speak so when he volunteered to join the British Navy, my Lords of the Admiralty sent him to F.O.G.M.O. to disect, clean and assemble binoculars and periscope sights. His companion in this work was the chemist from Grasmere.

After the war was over and I was nearing the completion of my theological studies, David got in touch with me to inform me that the Bishop of California would offer me a parish across there. Very tempting, but I felt the challenge was here.

Naval Health Service

I needed some kind of combined theology and biology to sort out Kevin Robson. He had been granted a compassionate posting to F.O.G.M.O. from the battleship *King George V* from which he had never been home for over eighteen months, yet his wife was seven months pregnant. That is where I needed the biology instructions. Was there some kind of remote control in these matters or even telepathic insemination?

Kevin's naval lawyer came to see me.

'Robson forgave his wife. He rejoined his ship but found her in a compromising situation behind a fairground with a corporal, when he came on unexpected leave.'

'I'm sorry about that for Kevin is such a nice fellow and is certainly a good worker. He seems to have really become attached to that baby which isn't his.' I remarked.

'Of course you may not know but any child born in wedlock is officially the husband's no matter what the circumstances unless there is a confession,' advised the lawyer.

'Even if he had never been near to her for eighteen months?' I queried.

'That's how it is at present,' was the answer.

'Seems ridiculous to me. However, what can we do?' I asked,

'She has admitted to her husband that she is a prostitute and wishes to remain in that age-old profession. So he had decided reluctantly to sue for a divorce

In his way he still loves her and wants her but she is adamant that she will not give up her way of life. Naturally there are no known witnesses, that is eye-witnesses of any adultery or misconduct. What we must do is go and obtain a personal admission of guilt from Mrs Robson before two witnesses.'

Eventually the naval welfare people got in touch with me. Robson was a Roman Catholic and so with a logic understood in naval circles only, they asked the presbyterian minister and myself, an Anglican, to visit Mrs Robson in the hope that she would make an admission of guilt to us.

We plunged into the jungle of Scotland Road and found the house. In answer to my knock all the neighbours took station at either their windows or doorsteps.

Mary Robson released through her opened door a solid block of polluted air.

She was clad in a dull skirt which was surmounted by the filthiest vest I have ever seen and I've seen lots of them coming up from ship's boiler rooms.

The vest was arranged so as to allow one naked breast to repose in a triangular sling; an abscess being the trouble.

Her voice was pleasing and more cultured than we had expected.

'Good morning, can I do something for you?' she asked.

I explained who we were and what we required.

'Come in,' she cordially invited.

'No thanks,' said the presbyterian padre who had a weak chest and bad eyesight.

I felt that we would never survive the passage through the passage.

She insisted and as we were the supplicants we finally followed her into a living room. It was fairly neat and I noticed that despite everything she still had a large photograph of Kevin on her mantlepiece.

'Coffee or tea? Will you have a biscuit?' she asked as she struggled into a blouse and then a jumper.

'It all began on June 12th,' she confided.

That happens to be my birthday.

We listened to her story. She was frank and yet very pleasant and tried to save us embarrassment. We got all the information we required although we had warned her that in the event of her admitting adultery and prostitution and through her admittance, a divorce was granted, she would lose her naval marriage allowance.

Months later I attended the divorce court proceedings. Mary looked like a duchess, beguiling and without doubt attractive.

'Do you consider Mrs Mary Robson to be a suitable person to have custody of the children?' the judge asked me. Besides having the illegitimate child, she had a child to her husband.

Reluctantly I replied in the negative.

On leaving the courtroom I was about to descend the stairs when a soft voice from behind me said,

'Lieutenant Richardson, may I have a moment please?'

I turned. There was Mary approaching me. Was this to be an unpleasant scene especially as I had won the custody for her husband?

'Thank you so much for what you have done. I do appreciate it. I'm sorry it had to be so and, curiously I do still love Kevin. But I like my way of life, and he is away so much.'

'Come and have a coffee downstairs' I replied.

In addition too our normal naval duties we were required to do spells of fire-watching duties. On my way to perform this one night after ten o'clock I walked from James' Street Station to the Liver Building. Ahead of me staggered a woman. In my opinion a drunken woman is odious. She seemed to have great difficulty in maintaining an upright carriage. Apart from this woman the streets appeared to be empty, for since the murderous Nazi onslaught from the air the Liverpudlians did not venture out much in the darkness.

The woman crossed the road and reached the Liver Building. There she clung to the iron railings which screened the closed cafe below. As I passed her she groaned.

Being unsympathetic I was not going to stop when I realized that there was no odour of alcohol. I went back.

'Help me,' she said, 'I'm having a baby.'

I was shattered. I knew how to take grit out of an eye and stones from horses' hooves but the only experience I had of childbirth was when I was the child.

'Hang on', I cried in desperation and fled to the entrance of the Liver Building. A seaman was on guard duty. He knew me.

'Get someone from the sick bay as quickly as you can. There's a woman outside having a baby.'

'Good for her,' grinned the seaman, 'I've had four.'

Breathlessly I returned to her.

'A doctor's coming,' I reassured her.

She transferred her grip from the railings to my wrist. She had a 'spasm'! It was like being in the grip of an all-in wrestler. The spasms increased.

My wristbones began to crumble as did my nerve. I began to sweat and gasp and have spasms myself. This birth was proving rather difficult for me. I should have had a course in natural breathing. I did the pushing while she did the comforting. No medical help arrived. We both needed it. I was becoming exhausted.

In the dark distance I saw another woman walking in the wrong direction. She was like a lighthouse on a perilous reef. I transferred the labouring woman back to the railings and ran hell-for-leather after this other person. She saw a man in naval uniform running towards her and took to her heels.

'Help,' she shouted.

I caught up to her. She was distressed. I could not speak immediately as I was out of breath. One good thing was that this woman was well beyond child-bearing age.

'Help me, please. There's a woman down there having a baby,' I panted.

'Look after your own woman,' she fairly screamed.

'Please come; you'll be too late. It's not my woman. She's a stranger.'

I hurried back with her fearful lest a little newborn had already hit the deck.

The second woman proved to be a boon.

'Stop that taxi,' she cried as a vehicle approached us.

I hailed it and it drew alongside.

'Where to, boss?' the driver enquired.

The pregnant woman gave a cry as I answered;

'To the maternity hospital.'

When the driver saw that he was to have a three-plus passenger list he objected.

'Not in my cab. No way. I've had this before.'

'As a naval officer in wartime I can insist,' I said, not knowing if that was correct.

It worked. The ladies clambered in and the driver broke the speed limit as he muttered under his breath all the time. I hoped that the about-to-be-born couldn't hear him.

Within fifteen minutes of arriving at the hospital we learnt that the cause of all the trouble was a baby boy.

When I returned to Liver Building I questioned the quarter master.

'Hey, where's that doctor I asked for?'

'Sorry, sir, I didn't go for the doctor because I know what a skylarker you are,' was his answer.

Later I had the joy of knowing that the black-out baby received my Christian name.

My fame as a midwife spread and I had many phone calls from fellow officers asking if they could book me for nine months time.

Malcolm

'Ow, that hurt!

I had slumped to the fender box exhausted and leaned back against a stocking hanging there to dry and brought a heavy, brass candlestick crashing to my head.

I felt that childbirth was definitely not for me.

This made Ethel forget her spasms as her labour increased and while she tended me, Malcolm, still within the womb, laughed himself into a breech birth. Ethel didn't laugh in the hospital when Malcolm delayed his launch for forty eight hours.

Visiting Ethel after the birth I found that she had been too exhausted to be shown the baby. All that she knew was that it was a boy.

'Jack, ask the nurse if you can see the baby. I'm sure that he has a hare-lip.'

Early in her pregnancy she had opened the cutlery drawer to obtain a knife when out jumped a wee, bewhiskered mouse. The wee timorous beastie was no doubt terrified but Ethel's terror was greater.

As I walked with the nurse to the room where half a dozen babies lay in cots. I began to wonder if there was any substance in old-wives tales. He was sucking his thumb obscuring his upper lip. I expressed my wife's fears to the nurse.

Gently picking him up she gave him to me.

'Take him to your wife. Let her hold him for a few minutes, then bring him back.'

Joy and relief were written all over Ethel's face as she gazed at the perfect miracle that was Malcolm. When I visited the hospital the nurses had put a broad band of gold on our baby's cot and had written the legend 'Admiral Richardson.'

'Name this child,' the naval chaplain commanded.

'Malcolm John Frederick,' the baby's great aunt replied.

The place was HMS *Kernot* which was the only ship wearing two ensigns; the British White Ensign and the Belgian Naval Ensign.

Thirty four years later the archdeacon intoned;

'Man hath a short time to live. He is cut down like a flower,' as he cast soil upon Malcolm's coffin. He had been killed in an accident in Genoa.

The Reason Why

Two torpedoes struck the ship; one hit the engine room.

She was carrying members of the Combined Operations forces. Her davits had been strengthened to carry assault craft. She sank swiftly.

Malcolm, Mac my friend, bound to me with comradeship that was good and cherished, managed with twenty other souls to clamber into a life raft and for three days in the relentless heat of each day and the chill of each night, floated on a becalmed Mediterranean Sea. On the eve of the third day when the sun was setting and the sea an oily calm their eyes were cheered by the sight of land.

It was Tobruk, then in British hands. Those ashore

spotted the life raft and immediately despatched a boat from the harbour to tow the raft in.

Before it got half-way, from the height of the skies dived a German fighter plane which raked the life raft with bullets, killing half of the survivors on the raft. Making a tight turn the plane came back and massacred the remainder killing them all except two. The boat from Tobruk picked up the bodies and the other two and brought them to port.

Mac was dead.

He was a wonderful man but his main philosophy in life was that goodness was inherent in everybody. If he survived the first attack by that aircraft I wonder what he was thinking when it came back for a second murderous onslaught. I know what I was thinking.

This was just a culmination of serious, tragic, horrific events which battered the bastions of my Christian faith. Brought up as a nominal Christian and a churchgoer, I now was faced with so many things that militated against that faith. It now seemed with this last sickening bereavement of mine that if there was a God, He didn't care!

Was God a casualty of war?

Was God dead too?

I had lost my friends at Dunkirk. My cousin lost his leg and eventually his life at Dunkirk.

My steward, Stripey Southern, was a grandfather, ex-naval who had been called back to fight in the war. He was a good living man, cheerful and always ready to help. He was conscientious and besides being a splendid steward was a most efficient seaman. He believed in God and he loved and cared for his family, speaking daily with pride of his grandchildren. He was an unforgetable character in many ways but it was his sincerity which marked him off as being so reliant and genuine. He and I were only separated when he was drafted to *Jervis Bay*. The *Deutschland* immortalized *Jervis Bay* for the latter put up a most courageous fight against the pocket battleship; a fight against tremendous odds that won the admiration of friend and foe alike. When the ship finally succumbed to the superior weaponry of the German raider, Stripey, who was a very poor swimmer, sensibly clung to floating wreckage. The convoy was safe but at the expense of a valiant ship and men of valour and courage. For twenty-two hours Stripey and a shipmate clung to the floating stay and eventually in the Atlantic waters, cold and rough, Stripey could hold no longer and sadly, yet not with despair but, I am told, with a note almost of expectation and even hope, he said;

'Give them my love at home. Goodbye,' and slipped into the sea that was now his grave. That shook me.

As I have already remarked my first ship was *Hood*. I loved her and was proud of her. She was in a class of her own. To me she was indestructible. Before Mac died at Tobruk *Hood* had been disintegrated in the battle with *Bismark*. Two thousands souls had been hastened into eternity in a moment of time. That shook me. Later with Combined Operations, ships from Inveraray took in a raid on the European coast and the Germans employed flame-throwers. I saw some of our lads sizzled up. Their eyes were burnt out, their features gone; gaps where there should have been mouths. Some miraculously still lived but were now sightless. I spoke at length with our ship's doctor.

'What can we do for these? Would it not be more merciful if they had died?' I asked him.

'It's marvellous what can be done with plastic surgery these days.' he replied, 'We can build up their tongues so that they will speak again. We can remould their features but of course we cannot give them new eyes.'

This and many other seemingly cruel and senseless things assailed my faith to such a degree that I doubted, reluctantly, but doubted seriously. Not for days or weeks but for months.

At night I lay tortured in my bunk. I felt hopeless rather than helpless. How could God allow these things to happen? It didn't seem to add up or to relate to the Christian faith. Calamity piled upon calamity, atrocity upon atrocity and I felt that I could no longer believe.

As I tried to throw overboard my faith so I always came back to believe in God. The difficulty then became trust in the fatherhood of God, a God who cared. Guided, I now believe, by Him, I realized that I had been asking the wrong questions.

'If there be a God of love why does He allow this to happen?'

'Why have men thrown over God?' I should have been asking.

'Why do men not follow God? Why have men forgotten or turned a blind eye to the love of God?'

So I began right at the beginning, thinking about creation.

Why did God create?

Now this book is not a theological treatise. It is a book, I hope, of joy, of fun, of sorrow, of life and of many of the varied things that have happened to me during my ministry, and before, with the Royal Navy. This chapter is to tell, briefly, why I went into that ministry; to show that faith was hammered out on the anvil of doubt. I feel that every convinced Christian, to be really and truly committed, must have experienced doubt of one sort or another.

'Lord, I believe; help thou my unbelief.'

Going back to creation, I asked why God had created.

What was His purpose in creating? If I accept that the essential nature of God is love then I had to accept that God by His very nature was, and I say it reverently, bound to create an object on which to bestow His love. It is irrational to love something that cannot love in return and so, the Bible tells us, God made man in His own image.

'In His own likeness He made him'

It is a spiritual likeness that is able to love. However simply in order to love one must be able to withhold love, for love is not automatic. It cannot be commanded. It must be free. It must be the voluntary submission of the entire self. This means that man, created in God's image to love God, must also have the power, the melancholy power, to

105

reject the love of God and I knew that as long as man loved God and responded to that love by loving his fellow men and seeking to show others through his own life the love of God, then all would be well. There would be no conflict.

If, on the other hand, man was selfish, and selfishness is inward looking, and was not looking towards God then there must be calamity; there must be war.

God didn't allow war. He allowed man to have free will and God sorrowed as men forgot Him and waged war. We see this clearly in the story of the Garden of Eden. All was well and there was a wonderful communion between God and man until man, seeking to be on equality with God, that is looking at himself, seeking for something that was not his, being selfish, disobeyed the gentle discipline laid upon him and so separated himself from God's love. The origin of all wars lies in that primary disobedience.

All God's activities since then have been to bring man back to the realization that God still loves and cares.

So, through a valley of great darkness I saw a light. I could be a Mohammedan or a Jew and believe all that. My difference was that I saw the ultimate love of God, the unselfish love of God, the unspeakable love of God in the cross of Christ.

God did not spare His only son.

'God so loved the world that He gave His only begotten son.'

God bereaved Himself and sorrowed with those who were bereaved.

God the son suffered, and seeking that love and feeling myself to be very humble and unworthy, I knew that I could not keep the knowledge of this love to myself.

I had to give it to others. So I resolved as the war went on, and later when the bestialities and horrors of Belsen and Dachau were revealed, that I had to pass on to others the love of God, and give up my naval engineering career and enter the ministry and His service.

So on Michaelmas Day, 1948, I was ordained and began my ministry.

I am like St.Paul who said he was persuaded that nothing, neither life nor death, nor things present nor things to come, nor any other creature; and I add WAR, can separate us from the love of God.

So in my lighthearted musings in this book of varied occurrences all I want to do is to show you that I believe God is love and as every one of my sermons, without exception, were of the love of God, so I hope that this book reflects the joy of serving Him.

God gave us a sense of humour. I thank Him for that.

Sin Bosun

Behind Bars

After my curacy and subsequent chaplaincy to the Earl of Durham I was again with the Royal Navy; as a chaplain R.N. I was rather a unique bird, for besides being a Sin Bosun, I held both engine room and navigation watchkeeping certificates.

'Jack,' I was in the bath at the time, 'fancy seeing *South Pacific* tonight?'

The Reverend John Blease, R.N. extended the invitation.

'It'll mean missing dinner,' I objected, being always conscious of my stomach.

'We can have a snack at the Nuffield. Give you half an hour,' said John who was equally as keen on his grub as I was.

I was waiting to take up my appointment with Daring class ships but *Duchess* which I was to join, was somewhere in mid ocean. Consequently I was kicking my heels in Portsmouth Barracks.

'You go in and order two ham omelettes. I'm just popping into the heads to see an Indian about a blanket,' said John indicating that he was about to answer a call of nature.

The cafeteria was crowded. I elbowed my way to the bar and ordered the omelettes. Bearing two plates I looked for table accommodation. All were fully occupied except one at which sat a gentleman in civvies and an elderly lady who I later learnt was his mother.

'May my friend and I join you at this table?' I requested.

'Certainly,' came the courteous reply.

I was also in civilian clothes. Soon I was in conversation with the man opposite to me. He did not know that I was a clergyman but the conversation drifted from pleasantries to serious religious topics. He aired his views in a definite manner but in my opinion was 'up the pole'. I hastened to correct him and instruct him and finally awarded him the following accolade;

'You wouldn't make a bad sunday school teacher.'

John returned. As he was pumping ship he had met an old shipmate and had chatted at length in the toilets. Finally when my omelette was consumed and his looked like a limp discus, he spotted me at the table.

'Hello,' he said heartily to my table mate. 'You two met? This is Jack Richardson; this is the next Chaplain of the Fleet!'

The commodore was a mobile, heavy black beard. I know of no one who knew if he had any features. I'm sure that his nanny must have had difficulty even in those early days distinguishing him from his woolly toys. When he spoke one looked round for a dummy.

'Padre,' his voice seemed to come through a sieve. 'Come into my office. I need to speak with you.'

His voice seemed to be friendly. It was difficult to tell otherwise as even his eyebrows conspired with his fungus and obliterated his optics. Like an Old English sheepdog he walked beside me. Seated behind his desk he removed his cap.

He was completely bald.

'Have you ever been in prison?' he asked me.

My guilty self examined myself. As far as I knew all my previous misdemeanours lay undetected. What had I done? I had told the future Chaplain of the Fleet that he would make a second-rate sunday school teacher; I had mistaken an admiral for a spiritualist and had stood up to toast the Queen in the *Victory* wardroom. Hardly enough to warrant incarceration.

'Not yet, sir'

I endeavoured to be lighthearted although I could already feel the shackles around my ankles.

'I understand that you are waiting to join *Duchess*.'

'Yes sir,' I affirmed.

'In that case you should be here for about three weeks.' he reckoned.

'Yes sir,' I agreed.

Three weeks with remission for good behaviour wouldn't be too bad!

'The padre at Detention Quarters has gone sick on leave. He really needs a rest. Would you care to take spiritual charge of D.Q.'s until you join *Duchess*?' he asked, knowing full well that I couldn't refuse.

At 1730, five thirty p.m. to landlubbers, I stood outside the massive, studded door. I rang a bell. A small hatch opened at eye level and a beak was pushed through.

Was it a hawk or a vulture? It could have been either, it seemed ready to pounce.

'It's the padre; let him in.'

I took a long, lingering look at the free world. The evening was beginning to yield to darkness. The lights of Pompey began to beckon the sailors to nightlife and fun. I heard laughter, probably from someone homeward bound, and began to yearn with appreciation for the simple things of everyday life.

As the heavy door swung open I thought of the Rubicon and looked up expecting to see the warning to all who would pass through this portal to abandon hope.

The Royal Marine sergeant was a most friendly person. Breaking step so that I could keep up with him he kindly shepherded me to the commander's office. Perhaps it was his friendly nature, his paternal instinct, that made him keep an iron grip on my arm.

'Ah, come in, padre,' invited the commander who was the governor. 'Sit down.'

'Sergeant, have some coffee sent in,' then turning to me, 'or perhaps a horse's neck?'

To the uninitiated a 'horse's neck' is brandy and dry ginger. I chose the coffee.

We began to talk. It was difficult to realize that this was the glasshouse; the prison.

'Sorry about the short notice. Can you preach tomorrow? Don't worry if you can't; I will. It won't be the first time.'

'Oh, I'll be alright. In fact I'd like to preach.'

'There's one thing I must tell you, padre,' the commander said, 'don't be distressed if no one takes a blind bit of notice of your sermon and that there is loud talking going on. You see, one of their privileges is that while they are in church they are free like any other congregation and it's then that they swap views and news. They don't like it if you preach less than quarter of an hour. But don't worry, I'll be there to read the lesson.'

'I'm beginning to look forward to it. Have you a form of service?' I asked.

'Book of Common Prayer. Straightforward. There is one thing, though. They're allowed to choose one hymn. Through the grapevine they'll already know there's a new padre. They'll try to take the mickey out of you, but whatever hymn they choose let them have it.' advised the governor.

The prisoners chose,

'Oh, that I had wings of angels,
Here to spread and heavenward fly.'

I noticed that no collection plate was passed round. Maybe someone might have nicked it and the contents.

Monday was the first day of my visiting. The sergeant, knowing that it is difficult for rich men and R.M. sergeants to enter into the Kingdom of Heaven, sought to ingratiate himself with the higher spiritual powers by courteously accompanying me. Like St.Peter, he was keeper of the keys.

A key, as heavy as a kedge anchor turned in the lock of cell number one. As a privilege they were allowed to call them rooms. Timidly I knocked on the solid metal door and almost broke my knuckles. A faint suspicion of derision played about the mouth of my escort.

'May I come in?' The derision was no longer a mere suspicion. The sergeant was enjoying this. I was nervous.

'STAND UP, you ugly son of a desert wart. The bloody padre's here to see you. Excuse my French but it's the only language they understand. Wipe that grin from your face, you b.... He's all yours, padre. Leave the door open.' instructed the custodian.

There was no furniture in the cell except the bench which served as a bed at night. Whatever else had been in, for instance a folding flap which served as a table or desk, had been broken up by the inmate when he was first put there.

I stood embarrassed. What could I say?

'What do you think of the weather?' He hadn't seen any for weeks.

'Read any good books lately?' The only book he was allowed was the Bible.

'What's your name?' seemed a reasonable remark.

The transformation was immediate. The prisoner's face lit up. He didn't identify himself but said, as if I was a benefactor from the Howard League of penal reform,

'You a Geordie?'

'Aye. Where do you come from?'

'Wallsend,' he proudly announced as if it was some

Shangri-la

'Well, you've certainly come to the end of the wall here, or should I say over the wall?' I remarked.

He smiled.

'Padre, you may not believe this, but I'm innocent.'

In my later rounds of visits I discovered that every prisoner had suffered a miscarriage of justice. They all professed to be whiter than the driven snow.

'Innocent? Then how come you are here?' I asked with concern.

'I put in a request and saw my captain. He turned it down and I swore at him.'

'Just a minute,' I needed more information, 'Are you telling me that you got ninety days for simply swearing at the captain. They must have been atom-splitting words to get that. There must have been something more than that,' I suggested.

'Whey aye,' said Geordie.'Me face didn't fit. You knaa hoo it is. If they divvent like ye, ye've had it. The skipper had it in for me from the moment I joined that ship I was a dog with a bad name. Got a fag?'

'You know, Geordie, you cannot smoke. I'd get wrong for letting you. Anyway I have none. I don't smoke. But I'll do whatever I can for you. Leave it me.' I said naively.

Over lunch with the commander I brought up Geordie's case.

'As a Geordie I'm really concerned. He seemed to be such a genuine chap.'

'Is that what he told you? I'll tell you what happened. He had put in a frivolous request. When it was turned down he literally launched himself at the captain on the other side of the table. He was ferocious. As a result the captain sustained a broken nose, a dislocated shoulder and had to have hospital treatment.'

In the short time I had there I listened daily to the complaints of the unjustly convicted. It seemed to be a place more innocent and naive than a monastery.

When I left them I did not expect a whip-round but I was

the richer in experience!

Darings

After three weeks in Portsmouth I was on my way to
Malta by air to join B squadron Daring class ships which
was made up of *Duchess*, *Decoy*, *Diamond* and *Diana*.

Our ancient aircraft which seemed to me to be held
together by string and sticky-tape had landed at Nice. We
had experienced a violent thunderstorm and had explored
the depths of an 800 feet air-pocket. It was 0200 in Nice and
we were asked not to leave the airport buildings. The plane
needed two hours attention. Fearful lest I might tip up the
frail aircraft if I used its heads which were right aft I
decided to patronize the French toilets before re-joining our
plane.

Well settled upon the throne, I heard an announcement
in English instructing all our passengers to board the plane.
By the time I evacuated the narrow cubicle the lounge had
emptied. I hurried through to find the exit door locked. I
was busily looking for other means of getting to the aircraft
when a gendarme succeeded in getting in. He spoke French
rapidly. It was double dutch to me. He called and another
arm of French law joined him.

'Ah, so. You are trying to get out. But the door is locked
is it not?' the latter said in English.

'Yes. I must join the plane to Malta. They have just
called for the passengers,' I replied.

'But you are not English, yes?' he remarked, probably
misled by my northern accent. 'Yes,' I affirmed.

'Hungarian maybe.'

'No. I meant "yes I am English".' Do hurry or I'll miss
my plane.'

'One moment, please. How did you get locked in?'

'I was in the heads, the toilets, the cabinetto, the loo,
when the tannoy requested all passengers concerned to join

114

the plane.' I replied impatiently.

'Which toilet? Show us.'

I stood anchored at the toilet door by an obstructing gendarme while the most bulky of the two searched the cubicle. He removed the lid from the cistern and delved his hands into the rumbling depths of wetness which had a slow-motion filling mechanism. He peered low almost round the 'U' bend until, their search fruitless, they frog-marched me to the plane. After an excited dialogue with our aircraft captain, whose actual name was Cumulus, I was allowed on board.

After take-off the captain explained to me that drug and diamond smugglers often left their contraband in lavatory tanks to be collected later by their fellow conspirators. I wonder how many smugglers the French police had caught who were wearing naval uniform and a dog-collar!

I was born on June 12th. Since that day I have observed

the anniversary of my birth in places scattered across the globe.

In 1955 my birthday dawned, revealing the coastline of Lebanon. Beirut was *Decoy's* destination and as we moored there I saw the cruiser *Jamaica* tied up on the other side of the mole. Ronnie, my cousin, sailed in *Jamaica* and he knew that it was my birthday. Just before noon my cabin was filled by Ronnie's ample proportions.

'Hey, Jack. Lovely to see you. I heard that *Decoy* was coming in. Happy birthday. Counting them backwards now? Ready to come aboard for a drink?' he asked.

'I'd love to, but only sippers please.'

Jamaica's corporal of the gangway recognised me as an old shipmate.

'Hello, sir,' he saluted, 'Come down to my mess in half an hour, will you?'

The ship's postman also knew me. It was the postman who insisted on sippers all round. This entailed taking a sip of rum from each sailor in that mess. I wasn't too keen as I do not really like rum. What an admission for a sailor to make. It is much more sobering to drink a yard of ale. Sippers was the greatest sacrifice a sailor could then make and it was reserved for such auspicious occasions as engagements, marriages, births and birthdays. I took it easy without giving offence but was pleased when I finally returned to my own cabin.

In the evening to freshen up I had a shave that I did not require, a shower, and dressed in my white monkey jacket. A cocktail party was in progress of the foc's'le so, vowing strict abstinence, I joined it. With an orange juice in my hand I joined my fellow humans who included Alex Henderson, a British resident in Lebanon. I also told stories to Peter Reid of the *Daily Telegraph* which were never published. The evening was lovely, the air still and darkness had brought the city to a pattern of lights. Soon I was to make an unplanned excursion into those illuminations.

Most of the guests had gone ashore but Alex remained to

have dinner in the wardroom and to watch the weekly film. I had seen the show on the seamen's messdeck the previous Thursday so I decided to turn in to my little pit.

Soon I was fast asleep, dreaming no doubt of Northumberland's rolling moors and sandy beaches. I was oblivious to the remaining hours of my birthday and to the fact that the mail arrived on board. When the steward took the mail to the wardroom it seemed as if it was special delivery for the padre. Over thirty greetings cards had arrived for me.

'Evidently it is the padre's birthday. Let's take him for a run ashore. I know the very place,' suggested Alex.

I was hoisted out of my bunk, to dress again into my monkey jacket and they took me ashore to try and make a monkey out of me.

The 'very place' was a night club, the first such establishment I had been in.

This one however was steeped in legend and history and even at times this plush rendezvous of the plenty, the pimps and the prostitutes was a place of religious pilgrimage. At least that made my presence there legitimate. It was allegedly the cave where the three wise men rested on their way to and from Bethlehem. It is known as the Cave of Kings.

We settled at a table, four officers, Alex and myself. The drinks were set up for a birthday toast. I raised my glass as, from a door to my left, a long line of high kicking females danced behind me in single file. They all displayed ample but entirely bare busts. I was just in time to see a photographer rise from the floor in front of me to take a flash snapshot. I forestalled him by doing a quick rugby tackle and the bare beauties stopped their siren swaying and singing to watch sailors locked in a scrum on the deck, ignoring the luring of those beauties who no doubt hoped to tempt unwary sailors on to the rocks of spiritual disaster.

Alex had bribed the photographer to catch me with the sirens behind me. For safety's sake I moved from the table to a high stool at the American bar. Relaxing with a wary eye directed towards the dance floor I heard a noise from behind the bar. Turning swiftly I was too late. The persistent photographer had popped up and this time had his objective. Half an hour later he presented us all with copies of comprising pictures which displayed me among the hills of Beirut!

'That'll make a good one for the Mothers' Union,' laughed Alex.

'And for the Lord's Day Observance Society,' added my treacherous shipmates.

'Not so,' answered Jack. 'It's after midnight, so it's Monday now.'

'But not in the UK,' was the rejoinder.

Perhaps it is a good thing that the wise men now allegedly lie in Cologne having reached there after the hazards of Byzantium.

'Anyone interested in going to Damascus?' I asked on the lower deck.

The answer was overwhelming.

We hired taxis to take us. The journey was not very inspiring. The scenery was the most derelict and depressing, absolutely devoid of vegetation and trees apart from the odd green patches around wells and little settlements.

Damascus was different, at least to me. I was interested and knew quite a lot about its history. I made a beeline for the Street Called Straight and saw the place from where it is traditionally believed St.Paul made his escape down the walls in a basket. The whole town excited me with its mystery and air of antiquity.

The climax came when a party of us went into a mosque. The custodians were so hospitable and careful to show us all their treasures.

'Here is our greatest relic and treasure; the head of John the Baptist,' said our guide.

There preserved in amazingly good state was a head. Our guide told us that they revered John the Baptist as a great prophet who helped to prepare the coming of Mohammed. He spoke with quiet respect and conviction.

The sunshine of Beirut was soon exchanged for that of Genoa. I organized a visit to the Cathedral of St.Lawrence. It was a worthwhile visit despite what happened. I learnt a great deal about St.Lawrence. Above the main door of the cathedral was a large stone which depicted the dying agonies of the saint as he was grilled on a gridiron. It left little to the imagination for as one looked one could imagine the intense heat and torture.

Our guide was a young, rather pedantic, priest who spoke excellent English. Our party included petty officers and seaman who had been with me to Damascus.

'Now I show you the great treasure. Our gem which is priceless, a relic of relics,' announced the priest. 'The head of John the Baptist!'

We peered through a thick glass porthole set into an altar. All that I could see was my own head upside down.

'That's not John the Baptist's head. We saw that in Damascus. How many heads did he have?' a burly P.O. spoke out loudly and candidly.

The shocked priest defended his infallibility. Accusations got a little out of hand and ridicule was made of the head being in Italy. So heated did this become despite my diplomacy that cathedral authorities were called and we were asked to leave and in fact escorted out. How many clergy have been thrown out of a cathedral for just trying to pour oil on troubled heads?

Istanbul

The Turkish pilot had a huge box of king-sized blocks of Turkish Delight.

I drooled, for I love the stuff.

'Care for some?' the Muslim asked the Christian.

'Yes, please.'

'We call it "Egyptian Delight" because it was originally made in Egypt. Likewise we call turkeys "Indians" for they are native birds of India,' said the pilot who was a veritable fount of information.

He was piloting us on the Sea of Marmara towards the Golden Horn of Istanbul, one-time Constantinople.

We moored in the shadow of the palace walls over which bygone Sultans threw their unsatisfactory or worn-out wives and concubines. Across the water we could see the Scutari coast made famous by the 'Lady of the Lamp'. Behind us was the Bosphorus.

'Padre,' said *Decoy*'s captain, 'the consulate chaplain is coming on board this morning to arrange a wreath laying ceremony at the statue of Ataturk. I will want you to go ashore with him to the consulate. Take the engineer commander with you for he wants to see about some spares or other.'

Ataturk did much to liberate the women of Turkey but I wonder what he would have thought of the enterprise of a most attractive young, Turkish lady in a gift shop actually in Ataturk Square.

The commander and I had finished our tasks and had an hour to spare before our boat was due to pick us up. We wandered into the gift shop.

There she stood full-bosomed, behind the counter, her dark hair fringing her olive features. She was the Turkish equivalent of Venus but she had both arms.

She wore a woollen jumper of light brown wool with a dark brown arrow patterned into the design and stretching from her right shoulder to the centre of her left breast. Here a woollen target received the tip of the arrow and above the target was woven the slogan,

'Squeeze here'.

We looked at each other. The commander said,

'Dare you.'

Very politely I went up to the young hopeful.

'May I?' I asked… and squeezed!

A loud pipping noise was emitted giving an initial shock but causing laughter all round. The young lady knew her business for after we had spun our yarn on board the squeezing business pipped into a boom.

That evening the shore-side chaplain came on board as my guest. Like me he came from the cradle of English Christianity. He had been a master at an English public school and was now doing duties in Istanbul. He was a great fellow, full of fun and down to earth. He brought me an unusual but delightful invitation.

I was invited to have lunch with His All-Holiness the Patriarch of Constantinople.

His All-Holiness had twice been rescued by the Royal Navy during the Second World War. He was extremely tall and looked taller wearing a high hat and a long beard. He was of the most unforgettable characters I have every met.

The chaplain was to share the honour with me and he gave me this advice.

'When you go you will be met by his All-Holiness in an

ante room. Don't, with Geordie fervour, grab his hand and ask after his health. Don't speak a word.'

'By, that's going to be hard. Do I just stand? What then?'

'Wait until a servant comes in carrying a tray. There will be three glasses of water, three spoons and a dish of white substance. The Patriarch will take a spoonful of the stuff and wash it down with water. Then the servant will come to me and finally to the main guest which will be you.'

'And do I take this white stuff, too?'

'Yes, and the more you take the more you will please him,' the lying cleric said.

Things went as he had told me.

When the tray came to me it was a case of all or nowt!

Winding my spoon generously about the white, gooey stuff I rammed a goodly proportion into my mouth.

It was horrible!

I could see the smile lurking about the chaplain's mouth. The sickly sweetness lay in my mouth like a ready-mix cement. The water found it to be a hazard and ran back out of my mouth as it found the obstruction violated free passage.

Finally I gulped. The concoction fell like a lump of lead into my innards.

The meal was excellent and managed to camouflage the erupting sweetness which hiccupped in my stomach.

'Come and see our cathedral,' invited the Patriarch.

It was small but beautiful. The icons were not only beautiful but beyond price. The building was a sanctuary from the noise and bustle of the city outside. I felt the peace.

As we were leaving, the Patriarch stopped by the effigy of a young woman. It lay in a small recess which might have been a chapel, an elegant stone tribute to a young saint.

'This is our patron saint.'

He told me her name but I cannot remember it.

'She belonged to Egypt. Her father was a leader of the Alexandrian community and of course a heathen. His daughter met St.Mark and was converted to Christianity.

She grew to love Mark, who was then an aged patriarch of Alexandria.'

I looked at the stone effigy. If it was portraying a true likeness then she had been a most beautiful young lady.

'Her father exerted pressure upon her to renounce the new faith. After unsuccessful persuasion to leave the fold, he resorted to threats. He warned her that if she continued with these people of the "way" he would burn her beauty away.'

'His own flesh and blood?' I remarked, 'How could he do it?'

'They lived in cruel times but even I wonder how he could do that, but he did.'

The Patriarch hesitated. He was speaking of a saintly martyrdom.

'Bravely she wouldn't renounce her new found faith and her father carried out his threat. Heated iron bars were laid across her face. Her eyes were sizzled out and her features mutilated terribly. In agony she survived for a few hours then died. One can still see the burn marks on her face.'

I was puzzled by this last remark. Still see the marks? How? I scrutinized the effigy. The Patriarch touched a button and the whole effigy swung silently and slowly upwards to reveal a maiden in an air-tight coffin or container. Her vestments were well preserved and the parchment-brown skin which stretched across her skull bore darker marks which could well have been the burn marks from the iron bars.

I cannot describe how I felt.

I held my breath, for even breathing seemed profane at the time. Here was a moment that was sacred and solemn. Time had ceased to exist. I was here, yet centuries away, gazing upon the face of one who had looked at Mark who in turn had looked upon Christ. Here, time and eternity merged. I wanted it to last. It does remain until this day in my memory but also deep within my soul.

I was privileged. Only two people could operate that button. The Patriarch gave me something out of this world.

Otherwise Preserved

I survived Istanbul but only just, for I was arrested at the Black Sea end of the Bosphorus for straying beyond limits. I was held for two hours, then escorted to the pleasure steamer which was returning to the city. I saw the largest covered market in the world; still the largest despite the destruction wrought by German air raids. We sailed down to Alanya, still in Turkey where, so we were told, no ship apart from small boats had visited for over two hundred years. It really was primitive being 270 miles from the nearest bus stop. It was a pleasant break for us. When I saw the long, golden and empty beaches backed by small, green hills I could scarcely wait to get ashore and walk and climb. Sadly the beaches were too hot for bare feet and the hills were covered with small bushes which were alive with black thorn-snakes; not poisonous but irritating. I thrilled at the ruins of an old church allegedly standing on the site where St.Paul had preached. It was in the old deserted village and the surrounding debris was so high that one stepped directly from the outside track through the roof to get inside.

Eventually we sailed into Grand Harbour, Malta.

A fierce storm tore the Mediterranean Sea into millions of violently resisting and mountainous shreds which challenged any excursion into their raging torrents. So when *Duchess* sailed, the *Malta Times* reported that we had answered a distress call. This was not the case. We were bound for Palermo in Sicily. Immediately beyond the breakwater which sheltered Grand Harbour our ship bucked and reared like a stricken mare. On the bridge the captain took two sea-sickness pills.

'Padre, you should try these. They are actually to prevent morning sickness with pregnant women. I always take them.' advised the captain.

'Thank you, captain but I'm feeling fine,' I refused.

'Oh, but the weather is deteriorating fast. Steward, go to

124

my cabin and bring the padre a couple of my pills,' was his insistence.

They knocked me out cold!

I knew nothing until we arrived in Palermo. The severe gale had uprooted palm trees, leaving them absurdly waving their roots in the air. A huge sixteen storey building was a twisted puzzle of girders. Duchess had sustained quite a lot of superficial damage and one of the ships in our company had lost its funnel.

I knew nothing of the storm.

I enjoyed Palermo and the surrounding countryside. I took many walks with outward bounding conscripts but perhaps the most amazing was to the Capuchin catacombs outside the town.

'Oh death, where is thy sting.' The Capuchin monks evidently understood the sting to lie in the six feet of soil piled over the interred. What a serious impediment it would be to have to claw one's upward way through stones and soil upon the sounding of the Last Trump. The priority in the heavenly queue would depend upon the depth and density of consecrated clods between the darkness of interment and the daylight of the serene. The turnstile would have clicked and stopped by the time the muck of centuries was scooped away handful by handful.

The monks drew the sting. No interment into the bosom of receiving earth. When the mortal soul took flight from its earthly vehicle the vacated shell was disemboweled. What was left was then pickled in a special and secret solution comprised mainly of salt and then dried in the sunlight for a year and a day. The resulting prune was then placed in a coffin with a loose, glass cover and laid in a catacomb.

Many of the rich laity bought their places in the queue and gained this privileged pickling. Those who were not endowed with an over-abundance of filthy lucre paid to be hung in rows like carcasses in an abattoir. As I wandered among the bodily catkins I came across a reservation for women.

They hung lifeless, grotesque in their once white nighties

which now bore the dust of centuries.

In the middle of this ghostly corral hung one man. He was adorned with a massive hairy moustache which could have benefitted from a conditioner, and his bald pate was rather dusty. A pair of wire rimmed spectacles were fastened around his ears.

'What's he doing among all the women?' I asked our monk guide.

'He has been there for over a hundred years,' replied the monk, 'In life he was a midwife and now he is at hand should he be required at the Day of Judgement.'

I kept a pregnant silence.

A fully comprehensive health service!

The even poorer, desirous of some advantage, no matter how mean, on that fateful day of resurrection but being so poor that they could not afford to hang around, had their bodies interred in the graveyard adjacent to the catacombs. Their pickled heads were placed on shelves lining the tunnels. There must have been thousands of heads there.

Ramps had been constructed so that stiff limbs and rolling heads would encounter no hazards. Similar to the monastery at Carmel, we had to make a 'subscription'. Before we could leave we had to squeeze past the fattest monk on Sicily, who sat with his begging bowl at the narrow exit, refusing to move aside until the bowl resounded with pennies from heaven... or maybe for heaven.

Algerian Apparition

Two men sat in a railway carriage.

'Do you believe in ghosts?' one asked the other.

'No' replied the man... and vanished.

Do I believe in ghosts?

After all the experiences I have had; a poltergeist pottering perilously about my own house until he disturbed me while awaiting the football results, so it was bell, book and candle for him; a mysterious hand which continually flicked off the electric light; the exorcism of a ghostly, ginger cat and–well the recollections are legion–the answer must be 'YES'.

The experience I best like to recall took place in Algiers.

Dawn was reluctant on January 3rd 1955 as the grey shape of our ship moved towards the light that was beginning to disentangle the sea's horizon, and away from the uncertain shroud of mist which blanketed sleeping Malta.

For ten arduous days we ran and re-ran all the hairpin bends in the Mediterranean Sea, and after shipping enough water to float the Ark we slid quietly into unsuspecting Algiers.

With one eye on dividends, a cocktail party was given on board that first evening. For example, the head of Algeria's public transport expertly directed his drinks along the route to the terminus of his two-way bladder but by the time he left the ship he had arranged that six luxury coaches would be at our disposal to convey our ship's company to such places as the Sahara, Barbary Coast and the scenes of the North African landings of World War Two.

The president of the best club ashore, which boasted its own private beach, had, after downing our concoctions of chloroform and claret, declared us all to be honorary members of the club.

'Good evening, Padre. Nice to see you. Are you holding any services to which we would be able to come?'

During the course of the evening it had become apparent to me that the speaker and his wife, a middle-aged couple, seemed to prefer my company even though they were sober.

'Yes,' I replied, 'If you come on board on Sunday at 1000 you can stay for the service and have coffee with me in the wardroom afterwards.'

'Then we want you to come ashore with us tonight for dinner. Bring your two shipmates.'

My shipmates referred to were the engineer and electrical commanders.

I have never known a parson to refuse a free meal so true to form with a pious hope and rumbling stomach, I accepted.

Returning on board well after midnight our hosts, Guy and Nellie, invited us to have lunch with them at their home and estate some eight leagues beyond Algiers. Fortunately we were able to go and by high noon we were travelling over mountains and uneven roads which truly tested our sea legs.

The estate was vast, running into thousands of acres, with terraced hillsides yielding the vine for champagne. Before lunch we were introduced to Nellie's educated donkey.

'What are two and two?' asked Nellie.

The donkey contemplated a little, shifted its weight to its starboard side and nodded four times.

'What are three and three?' I asked.

The quadruped's baleful eye hated me.

It nodded four times.

'Padre,' Guy called me, 'will you keep your last night in Algiers free for me? I would like you and your companions to dine with us that night. In fact, I have a job I would like you to do for me.'

'What kind of job?' I enquired.

'I'll tell you when you come that night,' was Guy's reply.

Time and ten days 'fugited' by. I scorched in the Sahara and saw its corn is oil, visited the Barbary coast where the inhabitants treated us as equals, ran the gauntlet of Algiers casbah and preached to an assortment of nationalities who had come on board thirsting for the Word and the horse's necks!

I was also drinking at 9.30 pm on January 23rd, coffee and liqueurs after a delightful dinner. Round the drawing room fire sat Nellie, Guy, a French general, my shipmates and myself. Four boxer dogs claimed the territory nearest to the firelight's glow.

'Guy, what about this job you have for me?' I parted the haze of cigar smoke with my query.

'I will tell you after eleven o'clock,' replied Guy as he consulted his watch. Like all good hours lightened with fellowship and cherry brandy, the time almost outran the clock which seemed to be in a hurry to mark the hour.

'Now Padre, will you lay a ghost for us?'

I went spectral white and the spirit within me fainted.

So Guy began this incredible story.

'Many years ago my father inherited this vast estate including this house which is in the middle of the estate. However, he preferred the soft, warm greenness of the Cotswolds and wouldn't come out here. He appointed a manager and actually sold this house. He died at the age of fifty and I got the inheritance. I decided to come here and run the estate myself.'

We settled back to listen, for so far the atmosphere was relaxed was easy.

'We got married,' Nellie intervened,' before we had

intended to, and came out here an extremely young married couple. Guy brought me to see the estate and the house. I thought that it was a really lovely house and asked Guy to do his best to buy the house back even if it meant paying above the odds.'

'I offered the occupant a sum far in excess of its value,' Guy said, 'and was terribly downhearted when the owner turned it down. So Nellie and I had to endure the heat, smells and noise of the town.'

Guy enquired about the state of our glasses and replenishments were made.

'Imagine my surprise and utter delight when after six months the owner walked into my office and offered to sell us the house at market price, well below the amount he had originally offered. Although excited I was cautious. This is earthquake country and I at once suspected that an earth tremor must have cracked the foundations. So I had it surveyed. Everything was found to be in good order so we purchased and moved in.'

'I'll never forget our first night here,' remarked Nellie.

'After our first dinner we came into this very room and with the four dogs we had then, also boxers, we relaxed. We were so happy and everything seemed to be so wonderful.'

Guy took over the narrative.

'Then it happened. At precisely eleven forty-five the door from the hall opened. The four dogs rose to their feet and joyously greeted an invisible visitor who according to the passage of the dogs navigated diagonally across this room to that glass door that leads to the terrace. This door opened of its own accord, the dogs halted, the door closed and the dogs returned to the hearth.'

Nellie spoke.

'I said, "Now I know why we got this house at such a ridiculous price... it's haunted. I'm leaving now".'

'What a job I had persuading her to stay. I reasoned with her until almost daylight,' remarked Guy, 'and eventually she went to bed with every light in the whole house blazing. In the morning in the clear, matter-of-fact light of day under a blue Algerian sky the previous night's episode seemed to lose its terror.'

'Nellie, what did we see? Nothing really. Yes, two doors opened mysteriously, the dogs behaved strangely but we didn't see any actual spectre or demon.

'So Nellie agreed to stay and after all those years we are still here and our ghostly visitor is still doing his nightly perambulation.'

There was a lull in the story to enable us to absorb the details and to have a drink.

'Bring in Claude,' Guy requested Nellie.

Claude was the half-Arab, half-French butler. He was young and had only been in Guy's employment for five months.

'After I had begun work here,' Claude began to relate, 'I noticed that an elderly Arab constantly occupied the old armchair in the kitchen. He never spoke or answered any enquiry. I asked the mistress who he was and did he have her permission to be there. She supposed him to be the old butler. He had left before I took up my duties and I had never met him. So the next day when he was sitting in the chair I asked Madame to speak to him. She came into the kitchen and asked where the man was.

' "In the chair" I replied.

' "But the chair is empty," exclaimed the mistress. I could see the old man but Madame couldn't.'

Claude gave me a description of the apparition and the narrative now passed to the French general.

He was in charge of the French security forces in Algiers, which then was still French. He had visited our hosts to advise them on anti-terrorist measures. To completely inspect the estate took a full week during which the general stayed as their guest.

'My first night after dinner,' he began 'we sat here chatting and those four dogs were lying on the hearthrug. At eleven forty-five the hall door opened and a benevolent, elderly Arab came into the room. The dogs leapt to their feet to greet him and followed him across the room to the terrace door. He went out closing the door behind him and the dogs came back and quietly lay down.'

Guy intervened at this juncture as if a thought had just occurred to him.

'Jack, go and try to open that terrace door.'

I got up, went to the door and only succeeded in opening it after a series of tugs as it was so stiff and it groaned as it opened.

'Apart from our ghostly friend's operations that door has seldom been opened for years, yet when the Arab opens it, it swings easily.' informed Guy.

The general resumed his story.

' "Who was the old Arab?" I asked. "Arab? we saw no-one." '

'So I was told the story which quite frankly I did not believe. I determined to test it out. The following evening I positioned myself half way across the old Arab's path. At the appointed time things went according to schedule. The Arab arrived, the dogs did their stunt and as they approached me I reached out to grasp the old man but found myself grabbing at the warm atmosphere of the room. The smiling Arab was not tangible and, as the spirit moved him, continued on his way to the terrace. I tried the following night but the ghostly visitor again evaded my grasp.'

'Can you describe this ghost?' I asked the general.

He described it in similar terms to the description given earlier by Claude.

'Now, Padre,' said Guy, 'We want you to give our ghost peace and rest. Will you do it?'

My companions assured Guy that I would and with naval precision placed a chair midships and installed me as officer of the watch.

I sat waiting.

The chairs clustered around the fire seemed to be miles away. I felt a weird solitude; an uneasy tension. I was waiting for eternity to invade time, for the spiritual to manifest itself: for a visitor from beyond the grave.

The dogs slumbered with an occasional snort and the general drank with an occasional snort, yet the snorting seemed muffled, eerie and from afar.

The lights in the room were all extinguished save the small, flickering lamp by the fireside. Under the door I could see a thin ribbon of light which came from the hall chandelier. The outside world had receded when the unknown pervaded.

No one spoke.

I was scared.

Then from somewhere deep in the bowels of the house, echoing as if from a tomb, a clock tolled the quarter. I prayed that nothing would happen, but it did.

The dogs ran from the hearthrug and for the first time in all those years went through the doorway into the hall and out of sight.

This was unexpected.

I could feel my heart thumping and I was in the extremities of nervousness.

I gasped and then looked towards my companions. They were safely enshrouded in a distant but indistinct halo of light as if spectators from Hades.

No one spoke. I knew that they would expect me to follow the dogs.

With leaden feet I did not gallop into the hall but dragged my unwilling legs astern of me. Each step seemed to be a mile; each heart beat like the Last Trump. What would I see? Would I come face to face with a dead, but resurrected Arab? As if the veil of eternity was pulled aside, that hall was revealed with apocalyptic clarity.

Beneath the chandelier, which shone like a spotlight from the heavens, I could see the four dogs standing on their hind legs and resting their forepaws against...........NOTHING.

I could see the pressure on the paws as if they were leaning heavily on some central pillar or invisible person.

In panic my impedimented tongue stammered out an

exorcism. The dogs immediately fell forward upon each other in disarray.

We left Algiers the next day and after a further three weeks ploughing the Mediterranean we slid into Grand Harbour at Malta again. Our mail was brought on board.

A letter from Guy, written three days after our departure from Algiers, informed me that the Arab had not walked since the exorcism.

A full month late another letter declared that my efforts had been completely successful and a small parcel containing a silver bound bible expressed the gratitude of Guy's household.

My much treasured bible, however, was spirited away, perhaps by someone thirsting for the truth, or a plain, mean thief, or, and I'd like to think this, by a certain Arab who now had more time to read!

My friends kept up correspondence with me. Here are some extracts from letters from Guy and Nellie to me.

May 1956

I drove down the track from my house to the main road, as you know a distance of roughly one mile. The gate across the track was closed. Draped over it were the bodies of four Red Cross nurses and their driver. Their throats had all been slashed.

They had been on their way to the area devastated by the big earthquake further along the coast. This inhuman outrage is the work of the political terrorists who demand self-rule for Algiers...

July 1956
Dear Jack,

I know that you'll understand how I feel just now. I live in daily fear. Each morning when I awake I thank God that I am still alive. The atrocities in this area are unbelievable. Last week the French owners of the adjoining estate were butchered in their beds. When is our time coming? Please pray for us... Nellie.

September 1956

....My workers have fled the village afraid to live in the isolation here where the security forces seem to be so ineffective. Many of the village houses are now occupied by terrorists. There are constant skirmishes between the so-called Freedom Fighters and the French military but I'm afraid that the wrong side have the upper hand... My terraces of vines are neglected and it grieves me. I have lost almost everything...... Guy.

November 1956
Dear friend,

Like me you will be devastated to learn that Nellie is dead..... She could no longer endure the murderous conditions and the continual threats, the daily dread, the burnings and the slaughters.... I found her lying peacefully in her bed yesterday. I thought that she was asleep..... Guy.

May 1957
Dear Jack,

Your letters help me to retain my sanity. How I long for the peaceful acres of Britain yet I cannot leave here just now. I can see fires burning on my estate as I write. The vines are all destroyed. I have little left. Even part of this house is fire-damaged..... Guy.

October 1958

..... My house is now totally destroyed. I will have to return to England. When you answer address your letter to... Guy.

January 1959

.... Thank you for your kind offer. I will not make my home with you but will certainly come to stay with you for a while. I hope to be in London next week and I shall contact you upon arrival. I am only sorry that Nellie is not with me I will miss her strength and resolve.... There is now nothing to keep me here.... I have nothing but friends.... Guy.

Guy never reached me. He collapsed and died in London.

Diana

The southern end of Italy was our next destination. I was on board *Diana*.

The evening before we sailed into Naples our captain invited me to dinner in his cabin. After lowering my defences with a good meal he revealed the purpose of his hospitality.

Unfolding a chart upon his table he began.

'Here is Naples.'

His thick thumb stubbed the chart and then moved southwards a little.

'And here is Sorrento. Just behind is the mountain St.Angelo. It's only 5,000 feet. I want you to take a group of young seamen up that mountain tomorrow, going up the hard way, camping on the top and coming down the next day.'

'I'm sorry, sir I can't,' I replied.

He began to sense that the dinner had been squandered.

'Why not?' he demanded.

'I have already arranged to take a group of lads to Pompeii. The bus is ordered and the names taken,' I explained.

'What time are you setting out?' he asked.

'We leave ship at 0900,' I informed him. I had no desire to go mountaineering.

He was not to be thwarted.

He considered options for a moment and then decided.

'You'll be back on board by 1300. Collect your camping gear, catch the train at 1400 to Castel Namarra, then go up 3000 feet in the cable car and meet the others on the summit. I'll send Chesty Morris, the gunnery officer, with them.'

The voice had spoken. It was imperative.

'Look, lads, that's Douglas Fairbanks. Let's say "Hello",' I exclaimed hoping that my recognition was correct.

'We're from the British naval ships at present alongside in Naples,' I explained to the star.

'Delighted to have met you,' Douglas responded and introduced us to the glamorous young lady with him. He signed a few autographs and wished us well. We had met him on the long avenue that leads to the ruins of Pompeii. Our visit there was a huge success but far too short.

Too soon I was back on board being kitted out with a pair of iron-clad, ton-weight mountaineering boots, two pairs of thick stockings; admiralty, arctic, for the use of; a double-spined shirt, khaki knee-length shorts, a rucksack and a one-man tent. I set off for the railway station like a one-man band with billy-cans and utensils clanging in disharmony.

It was almost 100 degrees in the shade. The locals lay inert in their siesta no doubt agreeing that mad dogs and Englishmen go out in the noonday sun.

Two stones lighter I reached the terminal.

The dozy clerk either didn't understand English or he didn't relish the northern accent. I was clear, though breathless.

'To Castel Namarra, please,' I requested as I handed him my admiralty warrant.

He grew excited. He spoke very quickly and gesticulated wildly. Eventually he drew a little map and with ten minutes left to departure time it finally filtered through to me that I was at the wrong station.

Outside, not a taxi was in sight, but a skinny bag of bones reeking of his stable slumped in a semi-stupor in the shafts of a gharry.

'Quick,' I disturbed the geriatric custodian. 'Take me here', as I pushed the clerk's map under his nose.

He held it first one way and another as the precious minutes fled by.

As the minutes sped the gharry didn't. We moved at a snail's pace.

'Quicker; quicker,' I demanded without result. I began to fear that I may be charged with kerb-crawling.

Using the pidgin-Hindustani taught me by my mother I yelled;

'Gildie lou.'

Amazingly we broke into a walk.

I caught the train by the skin of my teeth.

To encourage me in this great escapade the Admiralty had issued me with a first-class railway ticket. The train was in motion when I reached the platform so I had to scramble into a third-class equivalent to a cattle-truck. The seats were hard wooden struts that ran from stem to stern. There was one seat available. The adjoining two seats were occupied by one twenty stone woman suffering from an overdose of body odour and with a cage of lousy hens on her ample lap.

The pervading stench from the hens mingled with her exuding mist of perspiration and I began to itch. I am quite sure that I had a plague of red-mite before I was released at my destination. The hens were going to enjoy a rooftop in Sorrento.

I was going to carry their parasites until my next bath.

The overhead cable-car was waiting. I was the only passenger.

The conductor had been an icecream vendor in Britain and from his Scottish accent, must have plied his wares around the docks at Govan. He fought for us in the last war.

'Welcome aboarrrrd,' he greeted me, 'I ken you're British; aye?'

I listened to his life story as we ascended.

'What's that trapdoor in the deck?' I asked.

'That's the escape hatch; like to see?' he replied.

Without waiting for my reply he removed the four heavy weights that held the door down and lifted it up. I was horrified to be gazing down into a bottomless pit.

I wanted to escape, but not through that exit.

We reached the railhead. It was about five o'clock in the evening.

The conductor gave me instructions.

'Aye man, just walk up this path for a canny distance, maybe a thousand feet and you'll come to a disused chapel. A kirk, ye ken,' he grinned broadly.

'Any houses there?' I asked. I was longing for a drink of water but the railhead had no tap.

'No hooses,' he was still grinning, 'it's the chapel of San Michaelle, built a long time ago by a hermit. Take care there as the path divides. Follow the right-hand track and it will be the camping place you want, ne doot but you won't see it until you reach the top as it is around the corner.'

I tried to imagine a corner on the top of a mountain.

'Cheerio and thanks for your help,' I said to him.

'Auld lang syne,' he grinned as he began to descend and I ascend.

It was a glorious evening. The high altitude air was sweet and clear. I could see the sweep of the bay, the smoke haze which clung to Sorrento and the volcano Vesuvius. The Bay of Naples was a clear as a map to my right.

I walked slowly because my boots were leaden but, happily, I often stopped to look at the wealth of wild and rare flowers. The turf beneath my embattled feet yielded soft and springy. So I attained the chapel of San Michaelle.

The doorway was devoid of a door and the narrow window slits of glass. An air of peace sanctified the place. I sat on a stone inside and heard the organ drone of bees busy in the roof and the eventide anthem of the birds. The mellow light of a westering sun warmed the place and I felt near to God and was constrained to pray. Laying aside my rucksack I allowed the tranquillity of this hallowed spot to sink deep into my soul. I was in touch with reality that passed beyond the time of Michael to the timeless Christ.

Here there was no constant hum and throb of the air-conditioning, no rush of daily routine, no piping of orders or the smell of diesel oil. This indeed was peace manifest; the water of tranquillity and I drank deep. Such moments are rare in life and yet, I believe, so necessary.

The solemn moment which belonged to eternity sped over too soon. Reluctantly I replaced the burden upon my back and stepped outside from peace to bewilderment.

Where was the division in the track?

Indeed where was the track? It had gasped exhausted at the chapel and like me had lingered but not come out. There was no sign of even a trampled weed. I was at the end of the trodden way facing an uphill climb to be determined by guess and by God.

The going was steep now. The flowers rejected the rarer air and left their margin by the chapel. At times I was forced to walk where the ground fell away sharply to depths of five hundred feet. The pebbles became boulders and the snow on the summit was beginning to claim its dominion.

I reached the top as the sun reached its horizon. For moments the panorama was breathtaking although I had little breath left to take. The shadows multiplied the mountains. The setting sun claimed the snow as its reflector and all the colours of the spectrum danced quickly before they died. Here was a miniature aurora borealis. This was a magic and exhilarating experience. I was in a new world. Far below the lights of humanity glittered like evening stars beside the darkening depths of the sea.

So very wonderful yet I was alone.

Where were the lads from *Diana*?

I stood aloft on a small cairn, crested against the skyline like a mountain goat.

'*Diana*, where are you?' I yelled full throat.

My voice bounced from summit to summit as did the answer.

Across the great gulf betwixt me and the next range of mountains came the call.

'Over here, Padre; where are you?'

141

'I'm up here,' I bleated.

Clear through the high altitude I heard Chesty's voice.

'You're up the wrong mountain.'

'What now?' I called back in despair.

'Go back to the railhead. We'll meet you there.'

I began the descent.

The way back was dark. No inspired, wonderful moment of meditation and higher thoughts now. I was terrified. It became a case of self-preservation.

The air had grown cold and a cloud hung low and visibility withered. I was fearful lest I fell over the chasms that I had passed on my way up. I longed for the distant scene, one step was not enough for me. No known way, no light to guide, I slithered, stumbled, groped and guessed until suddenly I was at the railhead.

I hadn't seen the little chapel on the way down.

There was no Italian-Scot to wish me 'Guid Neet' and no shipmates either. Alone and far from home I rattled the locked door of the station but it refused to open. I had to take the weight from my feet so I stretched full length on the dewy grass. It seemed to be hours before six shipmates materialized out of the darkness. Then began another two hours' climb to the top of St. Angelo.

I begged Chesty Morris not to remove my boots for I was fearful that my feet would come off with them. The men offered me a can of black things warmed up which looked like black beetles and could have been for all I cared, for I was famished.

The next morning I couldn't walk. Besides having mutilated feet, all my limbs had stiffened. Volunteers were requested to take me back to the ship by rail. Everyone volunteered, not out of the kindness of their scheming hearts but in efforts to avoid the hard physical descent planned for them. Two were detailed as my attendants and eventually, back on board, my raw feet were carefully uncovered amid a wealth of offensive but good-humoured advice from the doctor.

Sin Bosun

Midship Discomfort

We sailed for Toulon.

'Come and have dinner with me tonight,' invited the captain before we reached the French Naval base.

The invitation filled me with foreboding. When after the meal the captain unrolled a chart he seemed to me to be ghoulish; almost a Dracula demanding what blood was left in me. He wouldn't get any from my feet.

'No mountaineering for me this time, sir,' I ventured timidly but determined.

'Of course not, padre,' his assurance was too smooth.

'See here; this is the coastal road from Toulon to Marseilles. It's really beautiful and I want you to take a party of lads with you.'

'But I can scarcely walk. My feet are still skinless. You see, I'm wearing gym shoes,' I protested dimly.

The resourceful skipper had his answer.

'We've a dozen admiralty bikes on board. You'll use them.'

So it came about. The word had been spoken and, as in Genesis, it was done.

After breakfast, like twelve apostles duly sent on a pilgrimage, we mounted our steeds for the assault course.

An admiralty bike is built like a battleship; solid steel; immense displacement; unsprung saddles and back-pedalling brakes.

The coastal route is undoubtedly picturesque but it is also extremely undulating, with some ascents one in four. We screwed our backsides on the unyielding solidity of the saddles. Chains broke under the strain. We began to walk uphill.

About lunchtime we reached St. Cyr. Here was a blacksmith's shop, a bar and a toilet. The blacksmith spoke a kind of Esperanto with a German accent.

'Can you repair our bikes?'

He understood and undertook an inspection of them.

143

'Thees ees scrap. No good. ne pas.' he condemned them.

'Couldn't you just make them fit to get us back to Toulon?' I begged.

'Give him these fags, padre,' suggested one of the sailors as he proffered his duty-frees.

It was a wise move; it worked.

We told him not to hurry. The sun was warm. We relaxed under an awning sipping various forms of refreshment and eating the 'tiddy oggies' the ship's chef had managed to sneak into our lunch bags without our knowledge, for the oggies were of the similar build and vintage to our bikes.

The afternoon passed pleasantly until we realized that our cycles had no lighting equipment and that darkness would be upon us within two hours. There was also the custom of the French to drive of the wrong side of the road and in the darkness, especially with sailors at the helm, this could be disastrous. The way back seemed to be much longer than the way out and our bottoms rebelled against any contact with the saddles.

Finally we rode through the ill-lit roadtraps of Toulon's dockland and reached our ship. That night and for days I found it difficult to stand or to sit down.

Bottoms Up

Much later and on board a different ship we visited a Mediterranean port. Invitations had been sent out via the consul to the local British residents to attend a cocktail party on board to be held the evening of our arrival.

Among those invited was the Anglican chaplain. Upon berthing a hand-delivered note was given to me.

'Please convey my apologies to your captain as I am unable to attend your cocktail party. I know that you will understand. I have a huge parish as far as mileage is concerned, stretching along this coast for miles. I have a special church meeting some fifty miles from here so cannot come to your ship. However, I should like to meet you. Can you phone me in the morning?... Consulate chaplain.'

I arranged for him to have lunch with me on board on the Saturday.

He was a splendid chap, elderly, in fact a retired canon of an English cathedral. He was of the old school, gracious and pleasant as if he belonged to the *Barchester Chronicles*, with a wiry figure and snow white hair. His voice was rather high pitched but quite soft and he almost intoned every word. His spectacles hung around his neck on a chain and I never saw him use them. He had never visited a man-of-war before and appeared to be a little nervous in the wardroom which was so full of boisterous, young officers of a different era. He had teethed in the steam age while they were weaned on nuclear technology.

'What'll you have for a drink?' I asked him.

'I'm a lifelong abstainer from alcoholic liquors,' he timidly confessed.

'Not to worry. I'll join you with an orange juice,' I replied.

'Care to look around the ship now?' I invited after lunch.

Beginning at the helicopter hangar we visited the bridge, operations room, fo'c'sle and the forward gun turret. Finally we crossed the threshold of the petty officers' mess and he crossed into a new experience which may have been exhilarating for a while before tribulation claimed him.

For some reason, which I do not know, the president of the mess had not yet savoured the sweet nectar of his daily rum ration. After welcoming us, the president offered the canon 'sippers' and proffered a large bone-china cup of rum to the chaplain. Petty officers were very jealous of their right to draw their rum neat. The old cleric later confessed that he thought that the term 'sippers' denoted some form of soft drink like coca-cola. To everyone's astonishment, and the P.O's dismay, he downed the whole cupful at one great gulp.

145

He drained the lot and also his breath. He collapsed.

'Get the sickbay tiffy,' ordered the president as he sought to revive that stricken clergyman who had partaken of a surplus.

The sickbay attendant appeared and hastily set about restoring breath to the canon who was now purply-blue and his eyes were staring out of their sockets and there were almost panic-stations until he began normal breathing again.

He revived but was still out-for-the-count. We propped him in an easy chair. This usually pale-faced clergyman now took on a ruddy hue as he slumped, rather than sat, in the chair. He began to snore.

'Let's have a sing-song,' someone suggested.

A piano was screwed to the deck and the engine room artificer, who knew no music, hammered out various tunes. In my honour we sang 'Blaydon Races', then a Scots song followed by a Welsh ballad and were just concluding 'Danny Boy' in true ecumenical tradition when we heard a voice; the voice of an inebriated retired canon.

One of the petty officers had spent the previous night in the amorous but commercial embraces of a French prostitute. As a mark of his gratitude and no doubt guarantee of his continued patronage, he had brought her on board for tea. I do not know what a French prostitute, or indeed I hasten to add, any other of the same old and even Biblical profession should look like but this one looked so frail, rather like Dresden china, so demure and sweet that it seemed to be that she would be more fitted to be a housemaid in an English stately home.

'I'll sing you a song,' volunteered the canon with a voice that could now split the atom.

He stood up with an effort, hesitated, swayed, stumbled and sank to what should have been a regular position for him; his knees. As if performing a penance he shuffled on his knees to the knees of the prostitute.

Taking her hand into his and looking up to her dark eyes, soulfully he sang a lengthy love song declaring in verse and disharmony a love that knew no ending.

The lads roared their approval.

I thought that if I had deliberately gone about to set up this scene it could never have happened. Here was a retired Church of England canon, dead drunk, on his knees singing a love song to a French prostitute.

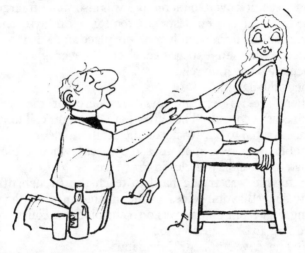

It was my turn to be embarrassed in the same port.

The consul invited the captain and I to dinner with him at the best hotel ashore.

The meal was ordered and while waiting we sat at the bar chatting.

My bladder signalled its top level and I had to take heed.

'Where's the toilet?' I asked the barman.

'Right at the end of this room. You can't miss it,' replied the English-speaking bartender.

I couldn't miss it. It was the only one.

Urgently I hurried in to find that the door had no bolt or lock or any other means of fastening it. Desperately I could not delay and had reached the point of no return when the door was pushed forward and a young lady stood there.

I began to fluster.

'Pardon moi, si vous plais,' I began

147

She took no notice.

'Allez, allez, pronto, at once; go,'

I tried all my faulty foreign languages to entreat her to retreat but she prepared for a long wait by lounging against the doorframe. It seemed as if the fountains of water would never cease flowing and under the constant gaze of the intruder seemed even to increase. I was also well off target!

She must have been desperate too for upon my eventual completion she immediately took my place and I fled.

'Phew; what an experience. You'll never guess what happened,' I began to relate.

They all laughed.

'There are no separate lavatories here for the sexes,' explained the consul. 'They are what you might call unisex. It is not normal to have locks on the cabinetto doors.'

Honour was redeemed to some extent when I took a busload of matelots to Arles in Provence.

My townie was trying hard to teach the French driver how to sing 'Blaydon Races' as the manner in which he was driving suggested that he was on a steeplechase course or at least doing an obstacle course.

'Why have we stopped?' I demanded.

'Because we go no further, yes?'

'Why not?'

'Because,' was the illuminating reply of the driver, 'all off.'

'We're not getting off here. We're miles from the town centre. Drive on,' I instructed.

'But no; the streets of Arles are too narrow. Coaches are not allowed,' he said.

'We are too boozed to walk,' said Stripey, which was not true, 'on your way, Frenchie,'

'No; no; I will get what you say "pinched"!'

'That's alright. This is the British Navy, and in any case the padre will take the blame,' some anonymous voice called from the back.

Either heaven heard my prayers or the gendarmes were having their siesta for a further two miles into the town we came to a beautifully gardened park.

'Drive into there and park,' I told the driver who obeyed the voice of the church but for safety's sake crossed himself.

We tumbled out of the bus adjacent to the site of the finals of the Arles *boules* championships. One of the finalists stood at least six foot four inches in his flat canvas shoes. His legs had the proportions of an elongated frog and his nasal billhook resembled that of Charles de Gaulle. His lengthy reach won him the title. He was receiving the congratulations of his compatriots when one of our sailors interrupted the cheek-kissing session.

'Our padre could beat him.'

Immediately the Eiffel Tower swung round and said,

'Ou est le padre?'

The matelot grinned earwidth for he now had a chance to expound in his halting French.

'Voila est le padre.'

The French amphibian cast a disdainful downward look of scorn at me.

'Ah; a tadpole,' he derided in English, 'I give you the challenge.'

It was arranged to play one end of two balls each.

He was about to throw the jack, not me, when Chalky White said,

'Hang on; it's got to be neutral. I'll throw the jack.'

I rolled my first ball. It sped along the swept, hard clay until it sweetly kissed the jack. I couldn't believe my luck but did not betray my disbelief but rather gave the Frenchman a meaningful look which being interpreted meant, 'Do better than that, mate, if you can.'

The Frenchman gazed in astonishment and muttered,

'J'ai le numero un.'

And played his ball. It came to an early terminus about a foot away from the target.

My second turn now.

Knowing that my first cast was pure luck I clasped my hands together in supplication. The Frenchman crossed himself.

God was on my side. Once again my steel sphere caressed the clay and drew alongside my first ball.

The Champion of Provence extended his frog-like gait in leaps towards the far end of the pitch. Carefully he surveyed the lie of the balls. Returning to the mat he played his remaining ball by throwing it into the air intending that it should rain down like brimstone upon my well placed steels. He missed.

'L'heure; l'heure; je suis en retard, Antoinette.'

So, *en definitive*, I became the champion of Provence.

I was extremely keen to visit the ruins of the place where the Council of Arles assembled in 333 A.D. to which the Church in England sent three bishops.

This was a most rewarding visit and made me proud to realize that the Church had been well organized and was thriving in England almost two thousand years ago.

After visiting the ruins I sat with a small band of our matelots at a table on the pavement outside a cafe. Along came others of our party who had not witnessed my international contest in the park. They joined us and I began to recount the epic. I swept my arm to emphasize and neatly knocked all the glasses to the deck

The resulting crash brought an irate proprietor to our table.

'Nous allons la ramasser,' I tried.

He answered in English, the vocabulary of Tilbury docks.

'Hey; you can't speak to our padre like that,' retorted Dusty Miller.

'Padre? Which padre?'

I was wearing an open-necked shirt.

'Him. Padre show him your identity card.'

I complied. The card bore a photograph of an uncertain likeness wearing a clerical collar.

The cafe owner looked hard.

'Pardon, mon padre. I will clear up. Have more drinks on me.'

So, a satisfied ship's company eventually bid farewell to the pleasant and friendly Arles where one Frenchman put his *boules* trophy on his sideboard and another his glasses in the dustbin.

'Bonjour tout le monde.'

Stone Frigate

The movement behind me startled me. My razor slipped. A thin quarter of an inch sliver of blood delineated the resulting cut.

I turned. There confronting me was a bloodhound, upstairs in my own bathroom.

Its baleful eyes fixed upon me. Its hanging jowls and wrinkled forehead looked huge and threatening. Regally it inspected me and made its opinion quite clear as it turned its hindquarters towards me then disdainfully withdrew its bulk from the room.

'Daddy; Daddy; there's a monster in my room,' yelled Christine.

I couldn't ignore this cry for help but as I reached her bedroom I was just in time to see the monster's huge, labouring stern descend the stairs towards where the bacon was frying. It spurned the kitchen and made its mark on the apple tree outside.

'Commander, we had a visitor this morning. It was a whopping great hulk of a bloodhound,' I informed Commander Barton.

He laughed.

'So you've met Pluto. He's a pet. No earthly good as a guard dog. He's too gentle.

He failed his police tests so we have him on the airfield.'

'Where do you keep the guard dogs?' I enquired anxious not to be inadvertently mauled either in a bathroom or outside.

'Guard dogs?' queried the commander.

'Yes. I saw prominent notices on the perimeter reading Beware; guard dogs.'

'There are no other dogs,' confessed the commander, 'Pluto is our only canine. The outside world doesn't know that of course.'

Pluto and my family became firm friends and to his credit during my commission with the Fleet Air Arm at Bramcote he sniffed out the body of a missing boy which had lain concealed in the rushes which grew thick along the canal bank.

Gamecock was a 'stone frigate', otherwise a naval shore establishment. It was a training centre for new entries into the Fleet Air Arm. Its unlikely location was in Warwickshire about as far as one can get in England from the sea, yet was about six minutes flying time to an aircraft carrier. The runways were of grass and the airfield was no longer operating as such, apart from irregular training flights and availability as an emergency airstrip.

This was my second experience with the Fleet Air Arm. At the time of the Munich Crisis in 1938 I joined *Furious*, an aircraft carrier originally built as a cruiser. It held the record for the fastest Atlantic crossing which was made during World War One. Her guns had not then been fitted, indeed they never were; she was at the disposal of Lord Balfour. He had to make a transatlantic dash to persuade or encourage America's entry into the war. It was of course top secret and I do not know if the crossing time has ever been bettered to date nor do I know the time it took. She was a lovely ship with a flush flightdeck.

I recall one particular incident which happened during my short service in *Furious*.

This was best told by a stoker afterwards in the canteen at Invergordon.

'We had left here in the dark and were steaming towards the last place on earth...Scapa Flow. It was darken ship and we were warned that the enemy, if we had one, could see the glow of a fag-end from a distance of three miles. I had the last dog watch.'

He paused to dribble beer down his spongy whiskers.

Wiping a massive hand across his mouth he continued.

'Suddenly there was chaos. All kinds of things were falling about. The ship jerked forward. I thought we'd run aground. I picked myself up from a grating and looked around. Chalky White had clung to a stanchion.

' "Bloody hell, the war's started," he shouted. "Chamberlain's made a mess of things in Munich."

'The killick, who's a clever bugger, suggested that we'd struck a mine.

' "More likely a torpedo," yelled Jonah Wales, as he looked around expecting to see water rise in the engine room.'

The stoker was out of breath. He needed refreshment. His glass was empty.

His pause was a definite demand to his listeners and his glass was replenished.

'Chiefie came down.

"What's up?," I asked him.

"Dunno" he said as he began to organize things.

"Damage control parties close up" was piped.

"Now I know we've been hit" I thought as the killick

began throwing his weight about. "Do this; do that;" when in fact he hadn't a bloody clue what to do.'

The stoker knew that the leading hand, a no-badge killick, was unpopular and played on this for a while.

'It was only when the first watch came on that we learnt what had happened.

'The destroyer decided to destruct or at least hitch a lift and tried to come inboard from astern. The enemy were supposed to be able to see a fag-end from three miles yet they couldn't see a whopping great aircraft carrier two cables ahead.

"Any damage?" I asked my relief.

"Dunno yet. Just have to wait." '

A seaman from Invergordon dockyard said, 'You were holed?'

'Holed? Big enough for the Queen Mary to sail through,' exaggerated the stoker, 'and do you know how we carried out emergency repairs?'

'Yes,' the answer disappointed the stoker who was just getting into full swing, 'you moved everything you could for'd, including the ship's company when you got to Scapa.'

The stoker intervened quickly.

'This lifted our stern out of the water and we covered the hole. The buzz is that we are going into dry dock at Chatham.'

Chamberlain returned from Munich and waved a piece of paper declaring 'Peace in our time', and *Furious* went into dry dock.

Captain Twiss, later Admiral Sir Frank and subsequently Black Rod, was commanding officer of *Gamecock*. He had suffered terribly at the hands of the Japanese as a prisoner of war. He was a godly man, genuine and efficient, a true Christian. and the more one got to know him the more one liked him.

As chaplain at *Gamecock* I was also responsible for hospital visiting over a wide area.

'Padre; I want you to go to Llangollen in Wales tomorrow,' said the captain.

'Right, sir. That will be a pleasant run.'

'But not an enviable task,' continued the captain. 'It's a

long story. The doctor will fill in the details. Be ready to leave at 0900. Transport has been arranged but check on it.'

Doc Mooney was also a fine fellow, a splendid messmate and most helpful to me and my family.

'What's my journey to Wales about, Doc?' I asked as I reached the sickbay.

'Ah yes,' the doctor replied, 'nasty little task for you. A seaman from Plymouth hitched a lift home to Llangollen on the pillion of a motor bike. They almost made it. They were only two miles from Llangollen when they crashed. The driver was killed. The seaman has sustained serious leg injuries; so serious that if his left leg is not amputated he will die.'

'So what do they want me to do; arrange a funeral?' I asked.

'No, no. The position has been fully explained to him. He refuses to consent to the operation and says that he would prefer to die rather than live with one leg.

'The doctors, nurses, social workers and his girl friend have all tried to get him to consent but without avail. His father and mother have been with him, indeed are staying at the hospital and they cannot persuade him. He is adamant that he wishes to die. You are our last hope. Go down there, Jack, and do your best. I'll say a prayer for you.' said the doc who was more used to dishing out aspirins than saying prayers.

Wally was of magnificent stature. He had been M.C.C. wicket-keeper in his younger days.Now he was the civilian transport superintendent at *Gamecock*.

He sat at the wheel of the naval limousine until I swallowed my cornflakes and then, dressed in my best uniform, I climbed into the front seat beside him. The weather was perfect. Soon we had left leafy Warwickshire behind us. We took our time, stopping for a mid-morning coffee at a quaint, old tea shop just over the border into Wales. It was almost noon when we found the hospital at Llangollen.

'Would you like to have lunch before we visit the hospital?' asked Wally.

'No. Let's get this job over with first. I couldn't eat my

155

lunch thinking about it. Go straight to the hospital.'

An hour and a half later I came out.

The lad was being prepared for the operation. I had been successful. It was hard to believe that our conversation had been fairly lighthearted and he made the task easier for me. He had even joked about Long John Silver although I think that a great deal of his lightheartedness had been a cover for his nerves.

'Phew, Wally, let's go into the town for some lunch. I'm famished. They offered me a meal in there but as the Admiralty's paying I'd rather have it with you'.

'How did things go, Jack?' enquired Wally.

'Very good indeed. He's having the operation. I think that eventually he would have come round to agreeing to have it. He really is a sensible, and brave, chap. It just took a little nudge from me. By the way, Wally, he asked me what would happen to the amputated leg. I left him ignorant. I'll never forget him. He was so cheerful that at one stage he had me laughing.'

Wally drove expertly into the town square and parked conveniently alongside the conveniences.

'Wow, Wally, after all that I must spend a penny. I'm fair bursting,' I remarked.

'Me, too,' said my companion.

The pressure within us relieved I led the way out of the conveniences.

'Mister, have you got the keys for next door?' the female looked at me urgently.

'What's next door?' I enquired.

'The ladies' toilet of course. It's locked . Hurry up please. I cannot wait.' she cried.

'But I haven't any keys. I...' her urgency intervened.

'Then has your mate got it?'

Wally drew his dignified six feet and fourteen stones to its full, impressive height and towering over the frailness of the little woman said,

'Madam, you have been addressing a naval chaplain.'

The poor woman went white and I'm sure that her urgency increased tenfold.

'O, I'm sorry. I thought you were the lavatory attendant.

Now I'll really have to go. What am I to do?'

'Have this one on me,' I valiantly said. 'Use the gents toilets. Wally and I will keep others out. Don't worry.'

Confident and at great speed she entered no-woman's land. Sheepishly when she came out she thanked us and said with both embarrassment and humour.

'I never recognised you...and I was a wartime Wren.'

Dessert..coffee and daffodils

The settee had lain for decades at the back of some purser's store but now it graced the padre's sitting room. Its Admiralty pattern covers held it together and contained the smell of woodworm killer. One cushion had permanently compressed springs so that occupants of the settee had a natural inclination to port. As we loved our dog we kept him off the settee and reserved it for special guests.

The captain's wife was such a guest and she shared this doubtful distinction with the instructor commander's wife.

I had sought to curry favour with my captain and had invited them to dinner at Anson House, the padre's married quarters. The commander was delayed and only turned up when the coffee was percolating.

'Got snarled up in a traffic jam. I thought I'd never make it so please excuse me,' apologized the commander who, when serving with a bomb disposal unit had been awarded two George Crosses.

Ethel entered carrying a tray bearing the coffee jug and cups, and humming 'It ain't going to rain no more'.

'You should see the traffic hold-up every night down the road towards Nuneaton.' I began, 'You know that junction about half a mile down in that direction....' I gesticulated by flinging my arm in an easterly direction successfully colliding with Ethel's tray.

The coffee pot slid forward and ever so slowly but inexorably rained coffee over the occupants of the settee. A warm, brown stain filtered through the new dress the captain's wife was wearing, to test the thermal underwear beneath. It made me think of when *Diamond* collided with *Superb*. With her bows firmly embedded in the cruiser's port side the *Diamond's* captain hesitated about his next move.

The admiral in *Superb* signalled,

'What are you going to do?

'Run a chicken farm', was the captain's reply.

With coffee baptizing my captain's wife I had to think of my future.

'Run a quiet, country parish a long way from the sea.'

From then on the settee was unique; it emitted a constant aroma of coffee scented woodworm killer. The dog never again wanted to go on it!

'Our chef is only good for making figgy puddings and "tiddy oggies",' remarked Ray Kingswell as we all sat together at the Ladies Night annual wardroom dinner. The captain's wife, in the place of honour, distanced herself from me and the coffee pot.

'Oh, he's not that bad,' said Marjorie, Ray's wife, 'but this sweet is rather sickly.'

'He is so incompetent that he would make a disharmony of peach Melba and all his meringues just need currants in to make them rock buns.' said Ray as he reached out to the floral arrangement. He selected a daffodil and to Ethel's amazement shook a little salt on it and began to eat it.

'I much prefer the ones with long trumpets,' he professed as he began to denude the vase.

'How come you eat daffodils?' I enquired, 'What about those tulips?'

'No to tulips; don't like them, but I love to munch marigolds, crush chrysanths and savour sweet peas.'

'What about dandelions?' asked Ethel.

'Well they're good for you and it was little flowers of the same kind that saved my life. When I was working on the Burma Railway as a Japanese prisoner-of-war our rations were insufficient to keep us alive. If we got sick we were often left to die. A couple of ounces of rice each day was hardly enough. The Nip who had charge of us was perhaps a little more human than the others.

' "Try eating those little yellow weeds that grow along the railway. They'll give you strength," he advised.

'Not knowing whether he was intent on poisoning me I didn't try them until things really got difficult. Out of desperation I thought, 'well even if they kill me it would be better than a slow death here, so I tried them, and it worked. They were full of nourishment and then from the same guard I learnt what I could safely eat.'

I knew what to buy him for his forthcoming birthday....a packet of seeds!

I have many pleasant memories of *Gamecock*. My Sunday morning walks before services to sort out my sermon thoughts, to Burton Hastings, a delightful small hamlet, and sometimes on to Withybrook where behind the altar in the church was the tomb of one of Guy Fawkes' conspirators who was stabbed in the back by his own sister, were not only inspiring but comforting and refreshing. Looking at Admiral Casper John, as he inspected, with great awe, – not because he was an admiral – but because he was the son of a famous painter, Augustus John. Travelling by bus to Nuneaton was a weekly experience. The bus was our umbilical cord with outside life but on each journey a passenger was requested to stand on the floorboards to prevent them from blowing up and filling the bus with dust in the dry weather or mud splatters in the wet. Of one local vicar who had served most of his time in the prison service and the other who decided that most of the Gospel stories were myth. Inevitably the blow fell. The government decided that for economic reasons *Gamecock* should close. Captain Twiss went back to sea; I was drafted to Christmas Island.

Scrooge never had a Christmas like this, whether it was Christmas past, present or to come, for this one never came. After receiving jabs against radiation, sunstroke, frostbite, South Seas insanity, rabies and ratbites and being equipped with anti-radiation jockey shorts and socks, the draft was cancelled. I was to join the Royal Marine Commandos. Big stuff; they only take the best!

Per Mare: Per Terram

'You're too bloody old!'

Colonel McAfee did not mince his words. He was known among the troops as Black Jack. He had another colonel brother, also of the Royal Marines, but I will not disclose his nickname.

Black Jack considered me to be sufficiently advanced in senility as to be incapable of completing the course which would earn my green beret.

'I'm not going to wear it unless I've earned it,' I replied.

'You'll wear what you are told to wear in this outfit, padre,' remarked the C.O. 'and I don't know of any other chaplain who has done the full course.'

'I'm sure there have been some.'

'They wouldn't be as old as you are though,' he was smiling through all this which was rather like banter than an official meeting.

'I was told that you were coming here to observe the course. That's good enough. Do you want to die young?'

'You just said that I was old; and who's going to die? I'll do that course and you'll present me with the green beret.'

'Right. You've no idea what really lies ahead of you. I'll take a wager on with you.'

'Good enough,' I agreed, 'What about a week's wages?'

'No fear; you would come off best. What pittance do you

get as a padre? Let's settle on ten pounds,' he suggested.

As I left the room he was grinning all over his black face; black not from skin pigment but from the dark hair that seemed to sprout from everywhere and shoot out horizontally from his huge ears. He was counting his chickens before they were hatched. I next saw him at church.

'I was thinking about you during the sermon. If you want to opt out of any one particular test just do so. I'll excuse you a couple.'

'And I was thinking about you,' I replied, for I had not been the preacher, 'I'm much younger than you are.' I won the wager but lost the stakes, for he never paid up.

I almost lost. I had transferred from Lympstone to Bickleigh on Dartmoor. Eighty feet up on the moor I stood on the brink of a sheer cliff. Other new recruits stood shivering at the top for it was a bitter day with quite a strong wind blowing. A cable was stretched from the cliff top at a steep angle to the far bank of a swift flowing stream. Looking over it seemed to me that it was a descent into the nether regions.

The exercise was to grab hold of a sling which had been well soaked in water in order to prevent it from seizing up through friction, drape it over the cable and launch out as if from the pinnacle of the Temple.

The most dangerous part seemed to lie in the landing. I watched carefully and saw quite a number of participants limp away or be carried away after landing. I looked over the precipice into the void beneath to try to reassure myself. The babbling of the stream seemed to assume the dimensions of turmoil and disorder associated with a roaring torrent. I decided to opt out.

A young recruit however had similar ideas. He trembled on the brink. His spotty face, blue with the cold, went whiter with fear making his spots stand out like currants in a suet pudding.

'Aa'm not gannin doon theor; nee way. Aa'm not gannin te kill maasell.' he declared.

Lieutenant Taylor considered this mutinous decision carefully and received inspiration.

'There's the padre watching you. He too is a Geordie. He'll be ashamed of you, won't you, padre?.

I looked for inspiration but found none. There before me was a replica of my own craven self. How could I judge the man?

'You can't get me like that,' the recruit said.

Then the northern nark looked at me with a crafty eye. 'I'll go if the padre goes first.'

I was scared out of my wits at the very thought of jumping off a cliff but was more scared to let Geordie think that I was scared.

'Right ho,' I cheerfully said. My smile was hypocritical.

'Nothing to it', I hoped.

I jumped. It was great. The thrill was unbelievable but I was pleased when in the twinkling of an eye I landed without mishap on the other side. If death is so easy there's nothing to be scared about.

Eight years later I married that craven Geordie. I looked him straight in the eyes and asked him if he had met his nurse bride while in hospital mending his broken ankle!

'Right, padre,' said the sergeant. 'Tomorrow we begin the speed marches. How's your feet?'

'What exactly do we do?' I asked.

'Tomorrow we do four miles in forty minutes.'

'Doesn't seem too bad,' I remarked. 'Should be able to

do that without difficulty.'

'Ah, but there's a snag. You'll have to carry full pack, a rifle and wear those nice heavy boots you haven't broken in yet,' informed the sergeant.

'Hold hard, though,' I objected. 'The Geneva Convention forbids me to carry firearms,'

'So it does. Then we'll just have to put an extra brick in your pack, won't we?'

They did and I discarded it the moment I was out of the sergeant's vision.

I completed the four miles in good style. The next day we had to tackle a six mile march within sixty minutes. The manner in which it is done is by walking up hills but running down hill and along level ground. After the six mile effort would come the ten miles and eventually the twelve mile final march.

A lorry was detailed to follow astern to pick up the dead and the dying. I spoke to the driver.

'Keep your eye on me. After a couple of miles I might need a lift.'

My gaunt bones, sparse hair and withered looks must have spoken volumes to the driver.

'Yes, sir,' he said, 'I would have done so in any case..'

After the first couple of miles, instead of being winded I gained a second wind. With a fresh spring in my legs I was covering the distances comfortably if not speedily. There were stragglers behind me. The sergeant dropped astern to hasten the laggards.

'Well done padre,' he said as he passed me, 'you're doing fine.'

My head expanded and my limbs became supple under the influence of pride. Such a vice is inevitably followed by a fall. Retribution was swift.

'Come on,' yelled the sergeant, 'You lazy bastards! Just look; there's a bloody old man doing better than you lot.'

That aged and bloodstained geriatric deflated.

The hazards of the course were over. The greater hazard of a night's celebration which was also one of farewells took its toll as noise of the aircraft shattered my sensitive ears.

163

Malta lay below us or rather as the plane banked Malta looked to be immediately off our port wing and not below. The padre's yeoman, that is his steward, was waiting in a jeep at the airport. His name was Patrick. He was an Ulsterman and had a red hand tattooed on his hand. He was a diligent, intelligent and capable steward.

'Have I time, sir, to call in at Valetta? I want to deliver a message.' he asked.

'Certainly,' I agreed, 'I'll stroll around a little just to stretch my legs after the plane journey. Care to join me for coffee and we'll have a chat and you can put me in the picture.'

'Well, sir, if you don't mind, I'll not join you for coffee. Should we say an hour's time.'

'OK.' I said, rightly guessing that there was a girl behind his request.

'Come in,' the C.O. called.

Colonel Jack Richards, better known in the service as 'Spur-of-the-moment-Jack', stood up to greet me.

He and I became good friends. He told me the trouble that had occasioned him to request for a padre. I knew that I would enjoy the company; 45 Royal Marine Commandos, based in the Middle East. It was just after Suez.

'When the green light comes on throw out that rope and shin down it. You will have six seconds to clear the helicopter. That leaves each man one second, OK.' said our instructor.

'Impossible,' said the doctor, 'I reckon on four seconds per man.'

The helicopter that I had to journey in carried the doctor, two sick bay artificers, the padre and his steward. It was forbidden to carry militants. We took off and seemed to circle Malta. Suddenly the green light shone, illuminating those of us who were already green with apprehension.

This was our first jump. The helicopter hovered. The doc took upon himself to throw out the rope and he speedily disappeared. Second from last was my appointed sequence. I shinned down the rope to find that it ended about ten feet above the ground and below me was a low stone wall. I would have dearly loved to have hung on, but fear made me lose my grip as my yeoman nearly landed on top of me.

'You'll have to do better than that next time, padre,' the instructor rebuked me.

In fact I became quite expert and used to look forward to the exercises. I learnt to drop from the helicopters, to keep a safe distance in the Troodos mountains when guerrilla hunting was on and to survive the rigours of the Libyan desert.

The flat bottomed landing craft wallowed its way to Tripoli in Libya. It reminded me of my war days with

Combined Operations. Its nose bluntly hit the shingle and we were out in a flash. Loaded into lorries we set off for an oasis called Tarhuna. It was about sixty miles into the desert from Tripoli. Nearby was a ruined Italian barracks. We lived in tents. I gave 'Padre's Hours' on sand dunes, had 'cush-cush' with Beduoin Arabs, and daily wrangled with an Arab barrow boy who called himself Jackson who had attached himself to our company. Every morning before putting on my shoes I had to knock them together to rid them of scorpions.

From out of nowhere the Beduoins appeared. How they navigate those uncharted wastes I don't know, but unerringly they made for the oasis. Some thousand yards from our camp they pitched their goatskin tents as they have been doing ever since the time of Abraham. They brought their camels to water to wash them taking great care not to splash themselves in the process as it was the season of Ramadan.

We watched them with great interest but they made no effort to communicate with us. To remedy this, four of us approached their site and stood, as is requisite, about fifty yards away from them. Eventually two of them came to greet us and were very friendly and asked us to share with them 'cush-cush' after sundown. Eight of us accepted the invitation.

'Let's take Michael with us if we can persuade him, ' it was suggested.

Michael was the only Jew I have met who served in the Royal Marines. He didn't look like a Jew and was very smart in his uniform.

'Michael, how about "cush-cush" with the Arabs tonight? Fancy it? We've been asked. We'll take you along.'

'Most certainly,' replied Michael, 'I'd love that.'

I wonder if he did.

'Cush-cush' involves the stewing of a complete animal, sheep or goat, with all its innards included. The skin is removed very carefully and used for all kinds of things from sandals, harness, camel seats to bagpipes. The stew is cooked in a large, oval stewpot suspended over a fire.

The eye is reckoned as the greatest delicacy and is given

to a chosen and favoured guest who must swallow it as the chief beduoin swallows the other eye.

There was no moon. The fireglow lighted our faces. The desert was as silent as the grave and the stars hung in sheer brilliance above our heads. The head of the feast looked at us all. Conversation was a little difficult but occasioned a lot of good humour.

'Doc,' I whispered, 'don't look up. He's fishing for the eye. I'll need you if he gives it to me.'

'And I'll need your ministrations if he hands it to me,' replied the doc.

The chief rolled back the loose sleeves of his robe and plunged his arm into the murky depths of the 'cush-cush'. He sorted around the lumpy blackness until he brought out an evil looking eye of a sheep. I wondered if the chief had an asbestos arm.

'Not me,' I prayed.'Not me.'

The wily Arab knew that the Jews are the chosen race. Michael went green as the eye was passed to him. He laid it on his palm. It looked at him. Maybe the sheep had been suffering from a thyroid disorder for the eye was staring and wide. Maybe mine would be if it was stewed.

The head Arab continued his underwater search for the other optic. He found it. Giving a gracious little bow to Michael, the chief swallowed his. Michael hesitated. Was there to be an international incident? Mike swallowed. All was saved – except Mike's digestion.

167

April first; fools' day. I had been fooled all night. I had beaten a track from my tent to the latrines. Weak, sick and pained I called out for Pat. He came.

'Get the doctor for me, Pat. I've been up all night.'

After a whole hour no one had appeared but when Pat arrived again to muck out my tent I asked him,

'Did you tell the doctor?'

'Yes, sir. I gave your message and he just grunted and turned over. I'll go again.'

Off went the faithful Pat who was having a respite in the desert from the demands of his woman in Valetta. Eventually the tall, broad figure of the doctor obliterated the morning sun from my tent.

'What's up. Jack?' he asked.

'Terrible gut-ache. I've had the runs all night.'

'I didn't come before because it's April Fools' Day and I know you for what you are. Let's have a look at you.'

He diagnosed appendicitis.

'Hospital for you, Jack. I'll see the C.O. and I'll make arrangements for transport. Get Pat to pack a few things. You should be away within an hour. Take enough things for a week or ten days at the longest. We'll be here when you come back.' he said.

The military hospital was in Tripoli.

My conveyance was a truck with a circular escape hatch in the roof of the cab. The driver was an Arab, for under our agreement with the Libyan authorities we had to employ a certain number of Arabs. He only knew two speeds; hell-for-leather and full stop. We achieved both. The dead stop, almost literally dead for me, came when we overturned on a sandhill. I continued the journey through the escape hatch, being catapulted unevenly so that my thigh received injuries.

I lay unconscious. The Arab vamoosed probably to offer prayers for my soul. How long I lay I do not know.

'Just put him here. I'll go and see if anyone is about,' the words brought me back to sensibility, or maybe it was the hard slab of a mortuary table that jerked me back to the land of the living.

My eyes focused and I saw two of our marines.

'Where am I ?' I asked

'In hospital, padre. You'll be alright now. Jock has gone off to look for a nurse.'

'How did I get here?'

'We found you. We were on patrol in a scout car and saw the overturned lorry. There's blood coming through your trousers but you seem to be in one piece.'

'Where's the medical documents?'

'What documents?' asked the puzzled marine.'

'I was on my way here as Doc says I've got appendicitis,' I replied.

'Don't know about them,' answered the marine, 'but here's Jock. Any luck?'

'Aye, there's a nurse coming.'

The ministering angel arrived.

'Boys, you shouldn't have brought him in here; this is the mortuary. Help me get him to a ward.' she asked.

The lads departed with my request,

'Tell Spur-of-the-moment-Jack what's happened.'

On a softer bed and alone in a ward the nurse looked at me.

'Let's see what we can find is wrong with you. Go into the bathroom and strip off.'

Displaying my manly form she examined my thigh. It wasn't too badly hurt, mainly skinned.

'Have you any pain anywhere?'

'Actually, I was on my way here with documents when we crashed. Our doctor has diagnosed appendicitis.' I informed her.

The surgeon was away playing golf and there appeared to be no other medical personnel.

'Where is everybody?' I enquired.

'Oh, you'll be well looked after, don't worry. The surgeon won't be long. We only have two other patients in the whole hospital,' she surprised me.

The surgeon was delighted to have a patient. He probed about, pushed here and there and eventually said,

'You have dysentery. We'll have to investigate to see what kind . I fear it is amoebic. I cannot treat your appendicitis as I would like, for as long as your dysentery persists, your wound after the operation wouldn't heal.'

They gave me a course of hypodermic therapy, plunging a gigantic hypodermic javelin into my side every so often. It worked, for to this day I still have that useless extra organ.

After a couple of days I asked if I may be taken to wherever the other two patients were. So they moved me into the company of an atheistic army captain who was due for discharge from the service and suffered from intense depression, and an attaché of the British War Graves Commission.

The army captain, despite his depression, had a kind of latent humour. One of his best efforts, directed at the War Graves man was this story.

'This is true,' he began, 'In our churchyard at home there is a grave with this inscription;

"Beneath this sod lies another" '

Curiously, years later when I was at Mitford, I came across a book which contained a photograph of that very tombstone.

I told stories of funerals to the Graves man which no doubt hastened the desire of the army man to escape to a happier existence. I tried to convert him but he was afraid that if he had a Christian burial I might officiate.

The nurse came in.

'Have a good breakfast, Jack; you're going back to your unit. The almoner will be in soon to see if you need anything.'

From the almoner I received some Maltese money, chocolate and newspapers from the U.K.

'What will you do when I go?' I asked, for the other two patients had previously been discharged.

'We are always ready for an emergency. It could happen at any time,' she answered.

Indeed it did happen shortly afterwards when there was a crash on the American Wheeler's Airfield near Tripoli.

The almoner returned.

'News for you, old chap,' grinning all over her face. 'The marines have left Tarhuna for Malta. I have arranged for a jeep to take you to Castel Benito R.A.F. station. You should be able to hitch an airlift from there.'

The driver of the jeep must have been the twin brother of the Arab who crashed me in the desert. He stopped the rocket-like progress of the vehicle by hurling it into a ditch. My head was gashed open.

'Not the hospital again.' I thought.

Along came an R.A.F. truck. They took me to the airfield. I sat there at a table sipping NAAFI coffee which had the same effect as chloroform, with a bloody bandage holding in the remains of my brains and a thumping headache. Along came the NAAFI manager.

'Are you alright, sir? You look ghastly to me. Care to go to the sickbay?' he asked.

'I've been,' I replied. 'What I want is a lift to Malta. How do I go about it?'

'Leave it to me. I can fix anything,' he assured me.

He didn't fix it.

'I'm sorry; there's nothing going to Malta today. We can always give you a bed,'

I would have settled for that, when in walked my own C.O.

'Hello, Jack; what are you doing here?'

I told him.

'Well I'm looking for a lift too. Let's go a little higher than the canteen manager and ask an air marshall,' he suggested.

I thought that he was being flippant, but using his exalted rank he saw an air marshall.

'That's fixed, Jack. There's a private plane going to Bengazi and they've agreed to go via Malta. We'll be with the lads tonight.'

We weren't.

At my request we flew low over Tarhuna, then landed at St.Andrew's in Malta. The unit had moved on to Cyprus!

My dysentery was still bothersome and Spur-of-the-moment-Jack suggested I scrounge a further lift to the U.K. This I did and ended up in Haslar Naval Hospital.

O.B.E.

Senile and geriatric I was finally released from the senior service and unleashed on an unsuspecting parish. I became chaplain to the Tyne Division R.N.R. Eventually I returned to my native county of Northumberland and was inducted as Vicar of Mitford. It was a beautiful, rural parish with a church originally built in 1135.

It had an interesting naval connection. Horatio Nelson's uncle Isaac was the incumbent during the last two decades of the eighteenth century. He was a firm friend of the family of Admiral Collingwood who lived at Morpeth.

Poor old Isaac met a watery end. He slipped from the moss covered stepping stones which spanned the river between the vicarage and the Plough Inn. He had been having more than his rum ration at the Plough and as he staggered back homewards he maintained an upright steady progress but the earth beneath him behaved like a heaving ship. Although dead when found it is said that he had a happy, fixed grin.

He built the vicarage in 1785. It was demolished in 1962 and a new, far too small parsonage house was built on the site.

Captain Jack Mitcalfe sat in this vicarage.

'Is that clock right?' he asked.

We had five clocks in the house and they were consistent in as far as they all varied. So we used mean time; not Greenwich but Mitford.

'Aye, it's ten to twelve,' I affirmed.

The captain had previously rung me up.

'I'll be passing your way tomorrow. Thought I'd like to look around the church. Will you be at home?' he had said.

Fearing that time would not allow him to fulfill his purpose of looking around our ancient church which had been built in early Norman times; burnt to the ground by

172

King John who was punished for this sacrilege by losing all he had in the Wash; allowed to fall into ruin until it was restored and the McLeod of McLeod installed as vicar, and received new life I hope when I went there, I suggested that we should pop across and do our looking.

'Church? What for? Had something done to it?' the captain surprised me.

I then realized that inspection of the church was not the reason for his visit. The clock pointers met. In the navy they made it noon.

'I'd love a sherry,' Captain Jack said. The coffee cups were still on the table.

'Now, I have something very important to say to you.' he began.

Fearing the worst I bribed him with a full measure and gave myself enough to bolster up my courage.

'Is your uniform in good order?' he asked.

Was the captain here to administer a private rebuke to the padre? My uniform was not in prime condition.

On the occasion of the admiral's inspection I had donned my best uniform, put on a clean cap cover, polished my shoes so brilliantly that one could have read the 23rd psalm in their gleaming surface, and attached my jangle of dazzling and impressive medals. I had parked my car in the parade ground facing the river.

The weather was atrocious. Heavy rain threatened my spit and polish, as I heard a cry for help coming from the murky depths of the Tyne. I peered over the guardrail but could see no one. I went back to my car and switched on all my lights and I saw a head bobbing about in the far side of the river. I dashed into headquarters and reported this, then grabbed a newly whitened lifebelt and a couple of fathoms of rope.

'Hey, you can't take that. It's all cleaned ready for the admiral.' shouted a leading seaman.

'It's not the admiral who's in the water,' I retorted as I ran.

When it was all over I returned to *Calliope*. My uniform was sodden and stained. The whitewash from the lifebelt contrasted with the dark blue of my uniform. The admiral was due to arrive in twenty minutes. The chief E.R.A. took my uniform to the boiler room to dry. I donned a cassock and surplice ready for prayers wearing only my underclothes beneath and a pair of shoes drawn from the stores.

After prayers had sanctified the proceedings and hopefully influenced the admiral I unrobed and dressed again into my uniform. It had the added aroma of diesel oil to the still discernable stains of the episode, so I tactfully avoided the admiral as he conducted his tour of inspection. I had to sit next to the admiral at the dinner. I hope he enjoyed it.

The man rescued from the river was an East German. He had been ashore drinking heavily and was busy saying a sailor's farewell to a local prostitute in the warehouse alongside where his ship was berthed when they hoisted the gangway inboard and executed a 180 degrees turn to port. The ship was a few yards from the quay when the seaman, hastily abandoning his amorous activities, took a running jump towards his ship. He missed his target and landed in the river. His ship was almost a mile downstream before those on board realized what had happened upstream. They fired a rocket, blew a blast on the siren, did another 180 degrees turn and headed back for their shipmate. He was taken by the river police to the infirmary where his master and first mate sat at his side until midnight when, against the advice of medical staff, they took him back on board and sailed.

Now I imagined that the captain sitting in the vicarage had come to administer a gentle admonishment to me about the state of my uniform on that night.

I was wrong.

His purpose had nothing at all to do with that.

Answering his query about my uniform I admitted,

'It's a bit tatty, but I can take it to the cleaners after the New Year.'

'You can always get another,' said the captain as if money grew on churchyard trees, 'Moss Bro's are sure to have some second hand ones available. Try them.'

I began a calculation. Soon the New Year bills would be

coming in and it was a long time before the Easter offering would be mine. So mentally I decided to humour the captain.

'The Queen wants to see you,' he suddenlysaid.

There was silence. I couldn't understand. I was bewildered. For once in my life I was stumped for words.

'Read this,' he continued and handed me a letter.

It was a command from the Admiralty instructing him to inform me, after twelve noon on December 28th, that the Queen had been graciously pleased to award me the Order of the British Empire, Military Division. This was in no way associated with my river experience.

I was dumbfounded. I felt a lump in my throat and tears starting in my eyes. I began to stutter. I did not know what to say.

'Now, let's drink to Jack, O.B.E.' suggested the captain.

'What's in the letter?' quizzed Ethel.

'Can I show it to her?' I asked.

'Certainly,' relied Captain Mitcalfe, 'But you must not inform other members of your family or the press until after midnight on December 31st.'

Then followed the longest four days of my life.

I bought a uniform which had belonged to an impoverished captain and required a certain amount of alteration. The four bands of gold had to be removed from the sleeves and the First World War medal ribbons were a little out of date despite my advancing years. These alterations evidently did not warrant priority and the uniform was not delivered in time for the investiture. Out came the old uniform a patch was sown on, the whole thing cleaned and pressed and it looked quite presentable. In a way I was quite pleased for that old uniform meant a great deal to me.

The great day was March 5th 1970.

The Queen noted that we were due to invade her palace so both she and Prince Philip went to Australia on March 4th, leaving the Queen Mother, that most gracious and lovable lady to face the ordeal of having the Richardsons at Buckingham Palace. On March 4th we entrained for London.

British Rail must have been warned of our travelling. King's Cross station staged a one station, one day strike. Our train stood at Finsbury Park for over half an hour before we were heaved off it with the information that King's Cross had 'blacked' the train. Finsbury Park looked like, and was to us, a foreign place. Being 'blacked' we received no help and had to lug our own luggage to the underground station. We stayed overnight with dear friends at Balcombe.

Early next morning Ethel got up and opened the curtains.

'By, there's been a heavy frost during the night', she said.

So heavy that it was in fact eight inches of snow.

By seven o'clock the blizzard had begun in earnest. It was impossible to be transported to Balcombe station. Mr. Hamilton kindly carried our luggage through snowdrifts.

'The train approaching the platform is the ten minutes past six, due to arrive at London Bridge an hour and a half ago. Please stand back.'

It was eight thirty a.m.

There was no standing back, just a concerted rush from the whole of humanity which had assembled on the narrow platform. Things were decidedly sticky in the carriage, and were evidently so on the rail for the train sugared up frequently until it was finally bottled at London Bridge station where it accomplished an irreversible coagulation.

The deadline for Buckingham Palace was ten a.m.

The timepiece at London Bridge had shivered to an early morning stop but my wristwatch heightened the panic by recording that ten o'clock was past history.

'Don't worry,' said the chirpy little Wren who met us at Victoria Station,' the investiture has been delayed for an hour because of the snow. Most recipients have been delayed,'

The Richardsons were in Buckingham Palace.

The sheep and the goats were separated; the family going off to port and I was shepherded along corridors to finally be confronted by a table behind which stood a line of gloriously arrayed attendants.

'May we have your cap, sir?' asked one of them.

'Yes,' I replied. 'Where's the heads?'

'Heads, sir?' queried one.

'The toilets', I enlightened him.

'I'm sorry, sir, but you don't have time to go. We're behind already.'

'And I'm sorry, too; for everyone's sake I have to go,' I insisted.

At a rate of knots I was conducted to the essential refuge and counselled to hurry. The waiting attendant chewed his finger nails down to the wick.

He galloped me to a long gallery which was penned out into sections for the various awards. Here a gentleman-in-waiting, in a frock coat, placed a tick beside my name on his list.

'What do I do?' I asked this undertaker's dummy.

'Well, sir, you have missed the rehearsal and there's no more time to explain', he said.

'I'm all at sea. I haven't a clue. Give me some idea, please,' I pleaded.

'It's easy,' he assured me. 'Simply copy the person before you; there's nothing to it.'

Feeling more comfortable and confident I began to chat to another recipient who was the Lord Mayor of York.

'This blizzard has certainly upset things. I came down last night and stayed at the Hilton. This morning all the taxis were off the road. Couldn't get a lift until a heavy lorry came along. I flagged it down.

' "Take me to Buckingham Palace and I'll give you a quid," I asked.

' "They'll never let me in," said the lorry driver.

' "They will," I replied, "I have special stickers for the windscreen."

' "Cor, can I have them for souvenirs?" asked the driver.

'So I arrived here in a lorry.' concluded the Lord Mayor.

'Ladies and gentlemen, will you please form up in the order of presentation,' began another gentleman in a claw-hammer suit, 'First, the Reverend John Richardson.'

'Oh, no,' I exploded, 'I cannot go first.'

'Why not?' he asked.

'Because I have to copy the man in front of me. I was held

177

up by the weather and missed therehearsal.'

'I'm sorry, sir, but the order cannot be changed,' I was instructed.

We were led in crocodile formation along rivers of corridors and through the rear of the throne room. We were proceeding down yet another gallery. I was panic stricken.

'John,' said an approaching admiral using my Sunday name, 'I'm sorry I'm late. It was the snow you know. You know what to do?' It was a question.

'I haven't a clue,' I admitted, 'I missed the rehearsal because of the snow.' I explained.

He took my arm and cut a channel to the nearest room.

'This was Lillie Langtry's room,' he began as if there was time for a history lesson.

'Now, just imagine that I am the Queen Mother,'

And so we rehearsed while the shade of Lillie listened.

The strains of the National Anthem were clearly to be heard as we finally made it to the appointed position.

I was head of the gang. The R.A.F. were guides and the Ghurkas were on guard. I was duly dispatched along the red carpet. Someone was reading a citation. It was so interesting that as I stood I listened to it scarcely realizing that it referred to me. I reckon that my best friend must have written it.

The Queen Mother radiated grace and assurance. She was lovely. Her eyes were warm and friendly as she fastened the decoration to the whopping great fish hook that had been placed in my lapel. Then she began to talk to me and she made me feel that I was the only person who mattered in that crowded throne room. She told me that not only did she know Northumberland but also knew the village of Mitford.

With a smile and 'You'll have your work cut out for you up there,' our chat concluded.

I was to take three steps backward so as not to turn my back on her majesty. Horror of horrors, I could not remember if I had mounted a couple of steps on my way towards the Queen. I groped my way backwards fully expecting to fall backwards at any time. It had all been level going and I soon reached the obscurity of another gallery where an attendant whipped my decoration from me.

'Blimey, I didn't have that very long,' I said.

'Would you care to make yourself comfortable and visit the toilet, sir?' I was asked.

'No thank you,' I replied.

'Then just go up to that door and you can re-enter the throne room. There is a reserved seat for you at the front.'

As I re-entered my decoration came back into my possession, neatly encased in a leather case.

It was an unforgettable occasion for both me and my family but the outstanding memory will always be that of a truly majestic yet charming lady, Elizabeth, The Queen Mother.

Epilogue

From battle cruiser to submarines; merchant cruiser to assault craft; Admiralty desk to destroyers; Fleet Air Arm to Commandos and aircraft carrier to auxiliary support vessel was all a sequence of new beginnings. Life is marked out with stepping stones and each step brings new visions and hopes and experiences.

So when the era of Sin Bosun came to an end so life in parochial duties began.

Even that led to another beginning; retirement.

Now I can enjoy writing, painting, delving into local history and develop my keenness for walking.

What when retirement is ended?

Death?

Surely from life's instruction even that must be a new beginning.

Yet our future is bound up with our past. In recalling my past I hope that apart from the pleasure I gain from it I will also continue to learn its lessons.

Life is indeed a voyage and sometimes the ocean is rough and sometimes benign. It is how we meet it that matters. I have met my voyage so far with a keen interest in my fellow voyagers and an absolute trust in God.

Glossary for Landlubbers

Jimmy the One

> The First Lieutenant, immediately responsible to the commander for the cleanliness, appearance and order of the ship. Senior executive officer over the seamen's branch. All executives are engineer officers with their brains blown out.

Pusser

> Officially in my day the Paymaster. Now known as the Supply Officer. Friendship with him can make life on board easier.

Pilot

> The navigating Officer; the last on board to know where we are going. Always running around in circles.

Sin Bosun

> The chaplain; padre; bish; who tries to keep God botherers from disturbing his numerous 'make and mends.' Like the engineers well endowed with brains.

Master-at-arms

> The most senior rating. Charged with the task of exacting discipline and punishing the offenders. The only rating allowed to carry a dirk. He needs it for his own protection. As much loved in the Navy as a Regimental Sergeant Major is in the army. Never known to go on leave; or to have known his father.

Jonty

> A lower form of life than the M.A.A. but with similar responsibilities, having the same parentage as the M.A.A.

C.P.O.

> Chief Petty Officer. Especially capable if in the engineering branch. If not then he is carried around by seamen.

P.O.

> Artificer in the engine room or a senior rating, petty officer, in other branches. Holds the comforts of existence in his hands.

181

Killick

The one who does all the work; a leading hand.

A.B.

An able seaman. The backbone of the navy. Well versed in all dodges; a lower deck lawyer.

O.D.

A general dogsbody who is to blame for anything that goes wrong.

Old man

The very opposite to O.D.; the captain who wines and dines and dishes out punishment.

Make and mend

Originally half a day free from duties for non-watch-keepers in order that they could make and mend clothes and do their dhobying. Has declined into a mad rush ashore for the nearest pub or woman friend.

Watches

First – 8 p.m. until midnight
Middle – Midnight until 4.0 a.m.
Morning – 4.0 a.m. until 8.0 a.m.
Forenoon – 8.0 a.m. until 12 noon
Afternoon – 12 noon until 4.0 p.m.
First Dog – 4.0 p.m. until 6.0 p.m.
Last Dog – 6.0 p.m. until 8.0 p.m.

Bells

Each watch begins with one bell on the half hour and this increases each half hour up to the end of the watch which will sound eight bells. The exception is the Dog Watch. At the end of the two hour first dog four bells are sounded and the last dog begins with one bell but finishes with eight bells. Hell's bells are not restricted to the chapel but relate more to the expressions of senior rates to lesser beings.

Stone frigate

A shore establishment especially favoured by Jonties.

Uniforms

Introduced, some assert, at the time of Nelson with a strong influence from the king's mistress, Mrs. Fitzherbert who would have liked rampant dolphins embroidered on the collars.

Number one... Best uniform with gold badges... for Sundays, high days and dazzling the gullible sex.

Number two... Second best uniform with red badges.

Number three... third best with red badges... tatty and fit only for the scran bag.

Other items of uniform have greater numbers.

Scran bag

If anything is mislaid it usually turns up in the scran bag, and may be redeemed by surrendering a bar of soap.

Dhoby

Laundry; washing; in my time carried out in the washrooms in a portable zinc tub which was also the bath. Of course, sailors use Tide.

Ship it green

To encounter heavy weather with rough seas breaking over the bows. Usually accompanied by a green complexion and vomiting.

Requestmen

To appear before the Captain's table in a hopeless cause.

Defaulter

To appear before the Captain's table for condemnation. Guilty before tried with the cap removed as a sign of guilt and penitence. The order 'off caps' is given by the Jonty who loves his vocation but must be wary of the resulting hazards.

In the rattle

A defaulter serving his punishment. All those in the rattle are innocent.

Ditty Box

More precious to a sailor than a woman's handbag. Contains all his precious belongings such as love letters, other letters, photographs and items he would like most to rescue in the event of a calamity. Cannot be searched without divisional officer's permission.

Horse's neck

An officer's excuse for drinking brandy and dry ginger. It is alleged to settle one's stomach in choppy weather.

Heads

Lavatories. In Nelson's day always situated in the bows or head of the ship hence the name. Now with so much fibre about they are scattered conveniently about the ship. A place for avoiding work or the Jonty.

Sippers

The greatest sacrifice a sailor can make; the donation of a sip, a small intake, of Nelson's blood, the rum ration. Usually given on birthdays but sometimes to weaken female resistance.

Rabbits

The quarry of all sailors worth their salt; contraband such as cigarettes and whisky, pusser's stores etc. Usually accompanied by the cry 'Tuck their lugs in.'